**HOW TO
MAKE A FORTUNE
FROM THE
BIGGEST BAILOUT
IN U.S. HISTORY**

HOW TO MAKE A FORTUNE FROM THE BIGGEST BAILOUT IN U.S. HISTORY

A Guide to the 7 Greatest Bargains from Main Street to Wall Street

RON INSANA

AVERY
A MEMBER OF
PENGUIN GROUP (USA) INC.
NEW YORK

AVERY

Published by the Penguin Group
Penguin Group (USA) Inc., 375 Hudson Street, New York, New York 10014, USA *
Penguin Group (Canada), 90 Eglinton Avenue East, Suite 700, Toronto, Ontario M4P 2Y3, Canada (a division of Pearson Penguin
Canada Inc.) * Penguin Books Ltd, 80 Strand, London WC2R 0RL, England * Penguin Ireland, 25 St Stephen's Green, Dublin 2,
Ireland (a division of Penguin Books Ltd) * Penguin Group (Australia), 250 Camberwell Road, Camberwell, Victoria 3124,
Australia (a division of Pearson Australia Group Pty Ltd) * Penguin Books India Pvt Ltd, 11 Community Centre, Panchsheel Park,
New Delhi–110 017, India * Penguin Group (NZ), 67 Apollo Drive, Rosedale,
North Shore 0632, New Zealand (a division of Pearson New Zealand Ltd) * Penguin Books
(South Africa) (Pty) Ltd, 24 Sturdee Avenue, Rosebank, Johannesburg 2196, South Africa

Penguin Books Ltd, Registered Offices: 80 Strand, London WC2R 0RL, England

Most Avery books are available at special quantity discounts for bulk purchase for sales promotions, premiums, fund-raising,
and educational needs. Special books or book excerpts also can be created to fit specific needs. For details, write Penguin Group
(USA) Inc. Special Markets, 375 Hudson Street, New York, NY 10014.

Library of Congress Cataloging-in-Publication Data

Insana, Ron.
How to make a fortune from the biggest bailout in U.S. history : a guide to the 7 greatest bargains
from Main Street to Wall Street / Ron Insana.
p.   cm.
Includes index.
ISBN 978-1-58333-364-8
1. Investments—United States.   2. United States—Economic conditions—2009–   I. Title.
HG4521.I343   2009   2009040682
332.60973—dc22

Printed in the United States of America
1   3   5   7   9   10   8   6   4   2

BOOK DESIGN BY TANYA MAIBORODA

To Melinda

and

Emily, Thomas, and Anna,

my life's inspiration

ACKNOWLEDGMENTS

In every endeavor that is called a book, more people are involved than anyone realizes. Even some of the people who have helped to shape the manuscript will remain forever unaware of their influence on the thinking, the writing, or the subconscious mind that absorbs, analyzes, or presents information, judgments, or flights of fancy to the author's audience.

Hence, it is impossible for any writer to acknowledge the contributions of all who make a piece of writing, fiction or nonfiction, come to life.

But that is hardly an excuse for errors of omission in recognizing all who have contributed to my growth and development as an author, a journalist, a financial professional, and a person.

I must first give great thanks to my wife, Melinda, who has borne an unusual burden in recent years as I sought to remake my life in a variety of ways, from 2006 through 2009. Her constant encouragement and support through a couple of career changes and some moments of self-doubt kept me stable, grounded, and secure enough to confidently tackle new endeavors in my life, without which I would be poorer in experience, both professionally and personally.

To my children, Emily, Thomas, and Anna, whose patience has been both an amazing sign of grace at early ages and a great help as I worked to complete the manuscript. Though disappointed by my frequent refusals to break away from the computer to get down on the floor and play, over the last several months they also encouraged me to finish quickly so that life could return to normal. Or, as my son just said to me as I was writing my acknowledgments, "now we can finally go back to the batting cages."

To my brother, Art, who always provides counsel, guidance, and excellent editorial advice. His assistance in shaping the book has been invaluable, as his early interest in writing was inspirational.

To my mom, Adelia; my sister, Lisa; and my wider family of in-laws, cousins, and friends, thank you for letting me skip out on a few gatherings so that I could put pen to paper.

To my longtime mentors, Doug Crichton and Arthur Cashin. They are both intimately familiar with how much they have influenced my life, in both the business world and in our real world. I consider it an honor to call them friends.

To my other longtime friend, mentor, and agent, Richard Leibner, who always keeps one eye out for me and one eye on me. His career and life counseling has been spot-on for more than twenty-two years. He has led me to other great people, such as George Hiltzik, who handles my radio work; and, more recently, Paul Fedorko, my literary agent, who found the perfect publisher, in quick time, to take on this project. I am, as always, in Richard, George, and Paul's debt. (And even though you're agents, please take that as a compliment, not as a percentage!)

To Harry Rhoads, Shayna Stillman, and the supreme professionals at the Washington Speakers Bureau. They provide constant encouragement to me, personally, and get me to stretch professionally, so that I am always finding new avenues of inquiry to explore. Harry Rhoads also provides the type of inspiration in life that is rare among professional colleagues.

To my editor, Megan Newman, whose patience, deft touch, and gentle manner allowed me to proceed with this book in a manner I felt most appropriate, as did her assistant, Miriam Rich. Megan's guidance greatly enhanced the arc of the advice contained in the book and its accessibility for a group of potential readers who have been burned by much of the recent investment advice they have received.

Many thanks also to Bill Shinker, who founded Gotham Books and enthusiastically agreed to publish the manuscript without a moment's hesitation. It has been my pleasure to work with Bill on my latest effort, and I hope it leads to a broader and deeper relationship over time.

—Ron Insana

July 21, 2009

CONTENTS

INTRODUCTION

I WANT TO ASK YOU A FEW SIMPLE QUESTIONS:

Do you believe the economy will be materially worse or materially better, in the next five, ten, or fifteen years, than it is today?

If you said "Materially worse"—and remember that this is about as bad as it gets—I would move to Montana, buy heavy arms, and stock a multiyear supply of canned goods, because we'll be back living in caves before long!

But if you said "Better," which is the *correct* answer, then, my next question is, "What are you prepared to do about it?"

Are you going to sit back and wait to see proof that the

worst part of this recession is over before taking the urgent and necessary steps to improve your financial future?

Or, like the savvy professionals I know, are you willing to use any spare cash you have, or redirect your current investment dollars, to take advantage of some of the greatest investment opportunities you'll see in this lifetime?

Despite the doom and gloom that you hear about day after day on television, radio, or the Internet, or read about in the newspapers, the world is NOT coming to an end. It's true that this is a difficult economy, probably the worst recession we've seen since the 1930s.

However, all recessions come to an end. And at the bottom of those recessions, where I believe we are now, are the single best values you can find in every asset class affected by the downturn.

Whether the roof caved in on real estate, or stocks came crashing down, or if hard commodities suddenly went soft, or corporate debt turned to junk, it really doesn't matter. All of that has already happened! That just means that the next big move, over the next five, ten, or fifteen years is UP, not down. Not the next five, ten, or fifteen minutes, but the next five, ten, or fifteen years.

Even the Great Depression eventually came to an end. And despite the Depression, AND World War II, the world didn't end.

Let me digress a bit and tell you a little story about the end of the world and making a market bet that it is just around the corner.

My longtime friend and colleague Art Cashin, a forty-five-year Wall Street veteran who has spent most of his career on the floor of the New York Stock Exchange, has seen many cycles come and go—good, bad, *and* ugly. Some so ugly that it seemed that Armageddon was truly at hand.

When training for his job as a broker, at the height of the Cuban Missile Crisis, Art's class of trainees was asked what an investor should do if the United States and Russia moved to the brink of a nuclear war and missiles were about to be fired from just ninety miles off the coast of Florida.

To a man, the class said, "Sell!" They immediately stood corrected. The correct answer, they were told, was, "Buy!" They should *buy* because, even if they were right, and missiles did fly, there would be no one left on the floor to fill their orders and they would lose no money.

If, however, they were wrong and the heightened tensions passed without a rocket being fired (as was the case in 1962), then investors could have bought stocks at panic-induced prices that had nearly reduced them to nuclear waste! And thus the move from nuclear winter on Wall Street to spring again would have been a very profitable one for those who bet against the end of the world.

Art makes the point a slightly different way. The Wall Street veteran has told me, time and time again, that if you bet on the end of the world, you need to be exactly right about the timing, because it happens only once. And even if you are correct, you will never be rewarded for being right!

Applying that lesson to the 1930s, and again in late 2008/early 2009, when the world also appeared to be ending, it would not have paid to make that same bet at the bottom of either cycle.

If you were still around, still solvent and prescient enough to pick up the broken pieces in the summer of '32, when the Dow Jones Industrial Average was 90 percent below its 1929 peak, you would have made a fortune.

In fact, when the Dow hit its rock bottom price of 41 in July 1932, it was at the same price at which the "original" Dow closed, on its first day of trading, May 26, 1896!

Imagine buying the 1932 Dow at 1896 prices.

Today, you can buy the "modern" Dow at 1998 prices. Or you can buy some banks and brokers at prices not seen since the early 1990s. Homebuilders are at bargain basement prices and industrial giants are trading at Lilliputian levels.

If, by chance, or by circumstance, you missed the run-up in real estate during this most recent (and historic) boom, you have an unusual opportunity to buy the house you wanted at anywhere from twenty-five to fifty cents on the dollar, depending on the location you desire.

Housing prices, measured by the most widely used barometer, the Case-Shiller Index, are down 25 percent on average across the country. Delinquencies and foreclosures are at record levels, and still rising! Bank sales and government sales of distressed and repossessed properties are surging.

I am not trying to pretend that this is not a painful chapter in our economic history. It is! It has been decades since Americans have encountered a period as difficult or uncertain as this one.

Six million Americans, or about 9.4 percent of the working population, are without jobs, and more than 16 percent are either underemployed or have removed themselves from the workforce altogether.

Economists suggest those numbers will get worse, maybe far worse, before they get better. But that has been true in every recession that I have lived through, that my parents lived through, and that my grandparents lived through. For that matter, it has been true for every generation that has come before us.

Most lived on to tell about it. I suspect that for us, this time will be no different, if history is any guide.

Mark Twain once famously said, "History doesn't repeat, but it does rhyme." We are in a rhyming phase of history that is unpleasant, at best, for most; unprofitable, at least, for many; and entirely untenable, unfortunately, for some.

But that doesn't mean that YOU have to be crippled by what is affecting someone else. Believe me, as someone who has spent a lifetime living through and studying the effects of booms and busts on the average American, I take no pleasure in pointing out that you can profit from someone else's pain.

But it is one of the hard realities of hard times.

There is a saying on Wall Street, however crude, that you "buy when there is blood in the streets." It is a rather cruel way of suggesting that when the going gets tough, the tough start investing again.

That's the message of this book. That at this time, no matter how bad things may appear, NOW is the time to begin accumulating the very things that have collapsed in value and that you fear will keep falling.

There are doomsayers who say that another crash is coming and that this has been just the tip of the iceberg. Sorry, *Titanic* fans. This iceberg's already been hit. The boat is foundering but you are not obliged to go down with the ship. It's time to save yourselves and move on with your lives.

It's also time to dive into the wreckage and not just salvage what you can, but turn a desperate situation into a more desirable one.

That is what smart investors do in every investment cycle. They jump ship when the great waves are cresting and they bottom-fish after the wave comes crashing down.

You can either sink or swim. The best choose to swim. Sinking is not an option, not if you have a life to live, children to rear, or a retirement to save for.

And unlike prior periods, in which great recessions or depressions were aggravated by unenlightened government intervention, this time there's a man from the government who's here to help.

The U.S. government has launched the biggest bailout effort in economic history! And, believe it or not, Uncle Sam wants YOU to prosper again. It's in his best interests and it's in yours.

Here are just a few examples of how the lifelines are going out:

- The U.S. Treasury is extending a helping hand—through many government-run, or government-sponsored, programs—to aid those who are least fortunate and who face foreclosure, homelessness, or bankruptcy.
- The Federal Reserve is taking heroic steps to fix our beaten-down and still quite fragile financial system, issuing a solemn public promise not to let our nation's biggest banks go bust and take the economy down with them. (This is an important point that cannot be over-stated! I will explain more later.)
- The Fed has spent untold trillions of dollars to prop up institutions, markets, and the economy as a whole, keeping this Great Recession from becoming another Great Depression.
- Banks, particularly community banks, are starting to

lend a helping hand, although at this juncture the big ones are doing so a bit grudgingly.

- And the financial markets, too, are beginning to cooperate. In recent months, they have recovered at least some of the $10 trillion lost in the last two years.

It's your job now not to wallow in tales of woe, but to pick yourself up and dust yourself off.

Take a good, hard look at your financial situation. Retake control of your financial future and take advantage of the bargains that the biggest bust in our history has created.

Use the biggest bailout in U.S. history to bail yourself out, you who live on Main Street. This is not just for the fortunate few who have spent their lives on Easy Street.

HOW TO
MAKE A FORTUNE
FROM THE
BIGGEST BAILOUT
IN U.S. HISTORY

1

THE SUB-PRIME PRIMER

As I said, I do not have much interest in looking back and agonizing over what has transpired during this most recent period of boom and bust, or in working out how it relates to prior periods of excess and greed.

That will be handled by others, and it will be the stuff of countless Ph.D. papers for countless years to come. This was the biggest credit, real estate, and financial market bubble to burst in the history of mankind, as market historians Jeremy Grantham and Marc Faber have suggested and documented. It is also the most complex episode in financial market history, so it will no doubt merit, and produce, countless tomes examining the origins, impact, and behavioral aspects of this bubble.

For my own account, I'd like to reduce the experience to something somewhat more simple, just as a point of reference for you to use as a reminder when preparing to reenter the marketplace.

The recent bubble was the result, as all bubbles are, of efforts by policy makers to limit the damage that was done when the Internet bubble burst in 2000 and the attacks of 9/11 threatened to hurl us into a very serious recession.

To keep that from happening, the Federal Reserve quickly slashed interest rates to a forty-five-year low of 1 percent. President George W. Bush passed a $1.4 trillion tax cut to revive the economy. Other nations, fearful that a recession could affect them, followed the Fed and the Bush administration by adopting similar economic policies.

Quite suddenly the world was awash in cash. The combination of rate cuts and tax cuts proved quite powerful. The U.S. economy, and the world economy, rebounded very quickly. From 2002 to 2007, every country in the world except for Zimbabwe and Venezuela grew at a faster than normal pace. It was the first synchronized global expansion in modern economic history.

With the excess cash building up, investors, burned by the Internet bubble, decided to invest in something more stable, such as real estate. As demand for housing grew, real estate prices started to advance rather quickly, creating a virtuous circle of rising prices, increasing demand, and still higher prices. This occurred as the economy grew rapidly and credit was both abundant and affordable.

Individuals who previously could not afford to own homes were given access to so-called liar or NINJA (no income, no job, no assets) loans. Everyone who wanted a mortgage could get one, regardless of their ability to pay. Some of the availability of this newfound credit rested on the Bush administration's philosophy of creating an "ownership society," in which all who wanted a home should be able to get one.

Some of it, however, was the result of predatory lending practices that took advantage of people without the economic literacy required to understand that the loans they obtained had features that would eventually trap them in a spiral of delinquency, default, and foreclosure. The rest was the result of outright greed and speculation.

As we grew rich on real estate, so did the rest of the world. Some countries also profited from the run-up in the prices of commodities, such as oil, copper, and other industrial materials . . . even commodities as unusual as uranium.

As their resource-related wealth grew, even more cash and credit were created. From Great Britain to Greece and from Chile to China, similar booms were taking place in real estate, commodities, stocks, and other asset classes.

So easy was the money that Wall Street created a new class of investment vehicles known as derivatives. Derivatives are investments based on underlying assets, such as stocks, bonds, commodities, or real estate. Some of them had strange acronyms such as CDOs, CDS, RMBS, CMBS, among others.

It was an alphabet soup of impossibly complex instruments that investors bought with enormous amounts of borrowed money, or leverage.

The trading in derivatives was just another way to take advantage of the credit boom and the bull markets around the world in real estate, commodities, and stocks.

With respect to the derivatives based on real estate loans, particularly sub-prime loans, financial engineers jumped on the opportunity to package these poor-quality loans and sell them as "high-quality" investments.

With the help of a nonstop Wall Street marketing machine and the complicity of the big credit-rating agencies, derivatives experts managed to gain triple-A ratings on loans that were, essentially, created from junk debt.

They sold these collateralized debt obligations, or CDOs (sub-prime loans served as the "collateral"), to many willing buyers, from banks and brokerage houses to pension funds and hedge funds.

The trouble was that the lousy loans remained lousy loans no matter how they were packaged or what ratings they were given. Once the real estate market went bad, so did the derivatives.

The crash in real estate and real estate derivatives caused over $2 trillion in write-downs among financial institutions holding these once highly coveted CDOs.

Trading in derivatives grew to be a business worth hundreds of trillions of dollars, an enormous multiple of the size of the world economy.

At its peak, the derivatives business was valued at about $750 trillion, compared to the global economy, which is $45 trillion in size!

With all that as background, the run-up in real estate became a cause for concern for policy makers who sensed that "irrational exuberance" had gripped home buyers and real estate investors, much as it did the buyers of dot.com stocks in the 1990s.

Home values during the earlier part of this decade increased at unsustainable rates, causing the Fed, and other policy makers, to fret about "asset inflation."

Eventually, the Fed, by raising interest rates and making money less available, caused the asset bubble in real estate to deflate. As real estate began to decline, it put pressure on the derivative investments that relied on rising real estate prices to maintain their values. That led to a death spiral in a variety of similar investments around the world.

From sub-prime real estate to sub-prime securities, and from crude oil to soy oil, markets for hard assets crashed around the world. That led to a bursting of all the related bubbles on the planet.

The credit markets collapsed. Real estate values plunged and, for the most part, continue their decline today. Global stock markets fell between 40 and 70 percent. Banks, brokers, and investment funds that trafficked in derivatives either went bust or nearly did.

Governments stepped in to save the financial system from ruin and their economies from sinking into a 1930s-style depression. As a result, never-before-attempted tricks of financial levitation were tried, creating trillions of dollars in emergency stimulus and insurance programs designed to stabilize individual markets and entire economies.

While we are not out of the woods yet, there are signs that the worst is over and that the historic actions taken by policy makers to fight this historic speculative episode are bearing fruit.

All that means is that it is time to follow the Fed, or certainly not fight the Fed, as the saying goes on Wall Street, and start investing where values have been created in the wake of this epic bust.

Diamonds are made from coal, and some investment jewels have been formed under the rubble of this collapse.

2

DON'T LOOK BACK!

(Well, Look Back a Little)

As I mentioned in the opening pages of this book, I think, from an investor's perspective, at this moment in time, it is almost irrelevant to rehash the details of a crisis that we all witnessed and experienced, in real time, and around the clock, over the last two and a half years. There was no escaping the grim news put before us every minute of every day. And much of it bore striking similarities to a couple of key crises of more distant vintages.

And yet most of it does not bear repeating or reliving, right here or right now.

That may come as a surprise to those of you who know my work on CNBC, have read my last two books (Mom, put your hand down!), have heard me on the radio, or have seen items I have published recently.

Over the last twenty-five years, I have developed something of a reputation for being a market history buff. I have been called CNBC's resident "market historian" both inside and outside the shop. It's true that I have dedicated countless hours to the study of financial market history. I find it a fascinating topic that can shed a great deal of light on current events, generally, and on current market conditions, more specifically.

Indeed, it may comfort you to know that, among my most important findings, and this is not unique to me by any means, the "boom and bust cycle" is among the most repetitive features of human behavior. The market pendulum, they say, swings between extremes of greed and fear, always going too far in either direction. So, in other words, this is just the down part of the cycles we experience on a regular basis in a market economy.

In modern times, we have had a financial market "crisis" about once every three years. In each case, most of us have emerged from it in good enough shape to go on with our lives as if it were just a bad dream. That's not true for everyone. The down cycles affect many, many lives for the worse. But, on average, almost all of us survive, and even thrive, despite these frequent financial setbacks.

While I normally recommend that most investors, even the least sophisticated among us, engage in a thorough study of market history before they begin investing, I'm not sure that it is time well spent right now.

What's done is done, and I will leave it to market historians to chronicle the details of our most recent crisis and to pass judgment on Wall Street's "bad" behavior, Main Street's "mania" for housing, and Washington's erratic and ad hoc policy responses to the "Great Recession" of this decade. (Okay, so I slipped some personal judgments in . . . sue me . . . everyone is suing everyone today, anyway!)

Still, it is helpful to know that we've been in this situation before, or at least some semblance of it. There are records of speculative episodes that date back to ancient Sumeria, where grain futures were bought and sold like crazy, just as they are in Chicago today. (Take two clay tablets and trade with me in the morning.)

In first-century Rome, citizens of the republic were found to have engaged in an orgy of speculation in publicly traded stocks.

In the 1630s, the Dutch, in a well-known cautionary tale about market manias, planted the seeds of a tulip "bubble" that has been the stuff of market lore for centuries.

The South Sea Bubble, the Mississippi Scheme, and the Roaring Twenties are the names given to manic speculative episodes in Britain and France in the eighteenth century and in the United States in the twentieth century.

They each had serious but not fatal consequences for the society involved. True, the aftershocks affected many, and in each case caused market and economic setbacks of serious import, but still the world continued to turn.

Japan's "lost decade" is the result of the bursting of their twin stock and real estate bubbles in the 1980s, leaving Japan in recession for ten of the last twenty years. Japan has yet to emerge from the longest bear market of modern times, but if one travels to Japan, as I have, a depression is not readily apparent on the streets of Tokyo.

The "dot.com craze" here at home describes our own, very recent frenzy for Internet and technology stocks. The 1990s were known as the "decade of greed," as Internet billionaires calculated their net worth with every tick of their stock prices. But after the inevitable crash, Silicon Valley suffered through a virtual depression, though the rest of the economy—post Y2K, post-crash, and post 9/11—held up surprisingly well.

It is important to be aware of market history and of the events that led us to our most recent bout of speculative excess in real estate, in credit, in commodities, and in emerging markets.

But it makes no sense to dwell on it. The world now moves far too quickly to reflect on what went wrong. There is time for that, in due course.

But this is not the time to sit idle if you expect to catch the next wave. Indeed, it's already begun. And it's certainly possible that the next craze will also lead to a buying frenzy in distressed assets that also ends in a bust. But it will be better to have invested now than never to have invested at all.

This has been true at the end, or near end, of every crisis prior to this one.

By the way, at the very moment I was writing the first chapter of this book, on May 29, 2009, the *New York Times* gave careful consideration to this point of view:

SOME SEE AN ECONOMY IN CRISIS, BUT THE INTREPID FIND BARGAINS

■

BY PAUL SULLIVAN

May 29, 2009 | Stanford L. Kurland, the longtime president of Countrywide Financial, once one of the biggest mortgage issuers in America, is now running PennyMac Mortgage Investment Trust—the firm that announced last week that it was raising money to buy more distressed mortgages. Not surprisingly, Mr. Kurland's critics accuse him of trying to profit from the downside of what Countrywide and other lenders wrought.

One thing is certain, though: Mr. Kurland is not alone in looking to invest in assets that were the hardest hit in the downturn, namely debt, private equity and securitized bonds.

The reasoning is straightforward, even if the timing is risky. Last fall, the financial crisis was so all-encompassing that many otherwise good investments were sold at steep discounts as people moved their money into the safest investments.

Now that a clearer picture of the economy is forming—albeit not a rosy one—affluent investors are among the first to look at areas where losses were made worse by excessive borrowing. Still, those who are investing are doing so cautiously.

Cautious or not, large institutions, professional investors, and high-net-worth individuals are buying varied classes of distressed assets that are appropriate for their level of sophistication, risk appetite, and degree of affluence. And remember, the "investor class" has historically been "first in and first out," and then first in again.

You can be doing the same thing, right here and right now.

Individual investors need not be excluded from earning their share of profits in distressed investments. There are many, and varied, vehicles appropriate for you to invest in. They include, but certainly are not limited to, physical real estate, such as new and existing homes, undeveloped land,

and partially developed tracts of land, upon which developers will eventually build new structures.

If you look in the papers or on the Web, you'll find deeply discounted *new* homes, financed by the builders themselves, at extremely low mortgage rates. You'll also find bank-owned sales of existing homes, short sales of homes by their owners, and government-run foreclosures.

There are mutual funds, exchange-traded funds (ETFs), real estate investment trusts (REITS), and some vehicles that have yet to be created that will allow you to return to the investor class and use professional money managers to select more complex investments in the distressed arena, which will offer you attractive rates of return without your having to select the securities yourself.

Compared with prior crises, this time around individual investors actually have a fighting chance to take advantage of the distress in the markets.

As I mentioned, there are many more ways today that allow you, and empower you, to participate in an inevitable rebound in the markets, be they real estate, stocks, bonds, or commodities.

The following chapters will explore the many opportunities that await you in the financial markets.

First, though, let me introduce you to a few individuals whose actions you may want to emulate. You may have heard of them, or you may not have. But in my experience, these are the pros who can guide your investment decisions by leading you along the same path they have followed over the course of their long and successful careers.

While I believe it always pays to study the past, a quicker way to profits, in this market, is to simply follow the pros . . . in the present.

3

DRESSED FOR DISTRESS

FROM THE *DAILY TELEGRAPH* (UK):

JOHN PAULSON BETS ON PROPERTY RECOVERY WITH NEW FUND

Monday, May 18, 2009 | John Paulson, the hedge fund manager who made an estimated $3.7bn shorting the US housing market ahead of its collapse, is placing a firm bet on a medium-term property recovery with the launch of a new fund.

Paulson & Co. is in the early stages of raising money for the new fund. In a departure for the firm, which tends to be more focused on running hedge funds, the new venture will be a private equity fund.

————

The aforementioned John Paulson was known on Wall Street for many years as a sharp hedge-fund investor with above-average rates of return. But unlike more famous investors, he is hardly a household name on Main Street.

However, in 2007, Paulson joined the ranks of original hedge-fund legends such as James Simons, George Soros, David E. Shaw, Julian Robertson, and Michael Steinhardt, or next-generation legends such as Steven A. Cohen (my old boss), Stanley Druckenmiller, Paul Tudor Jones, Eddie Lampert, and just a handful of others, by making a career-changing bet that vaulted him to the top of the hedge-fund heap.

Most average Americans find it hard to believe that the sums of money that hedge-fund managers have made are derived from legitimate work. But having worked in the industry, as well as having observed it, for twenty-five years, I can tell you firsthand that the work is mind-numbingly complex.

It's true that if you're right, your annual paycheck can dwarf the GDP (Gross Domestic Product) of some small companies. But it's also true that if you're wrong, you can wipe yourself, and your investors, out for good.

Many of the managers I mentioned earlier have had the privilege of taking home more than a billion dollars, personally, in a single year. It's hard to fathom, I know, when most people get by on a median income of about $50,000 in the United States, and far less in the rest of the world.

Most people didn't come to realize how much money hedge-fund managers were making until George Soros, one of the early entrants into the business, made headlines in the early 1990s.

George Soros, who famously "broke the Bank of England" in 1992, earned a billion dollars betting against the British pound. The profit he earned from pounding the pound made headlines the world over.

James Simons, like David E. Shaw, whose computer-driven trading strategies are guided by mind-numbingly complex mathematical formulas, earned $1.5 billion for himself in 2006.

Steve Cohen, known to many as the best stock trader in the history of Wall Street, is among those whose personal paychecks topped a billion dollars in only twelve months, along with stock picker Eddie Lampert.

But John Paulson's $3.7 billion personal payday in 2007 is the single biggest profit ever earned by a hedge-fund manager in financial-market history. His firm, Paulson & Co., made a whopping $8 billion in 2007, betting that housing would collapse, and the financial system along with it. Paulson took home almost half the profits.

Using a variety of strategies, Paulson made money by shorting sub-prime mortgage derivatives and financial stocks and by buying other arcane investments that skyrocketed in value as the markets plunged by record numbers.

Unlike almost anyone else in his business, Paulson pressed his bet the following year, and his prophetic vision earned him handsome profits again in 2008.

But as you can see, that is past history. Paulson is now betting that real estate will recover, and he's raising new money to take advantage of the opportunity. He has called the current environment for distressed investment "a $10 trillion opportunity." Hundreds of billions of dollars have been raised to invest in distressed assets over the last eighteen months.

Most certainly there is room for you to capture a portion of those profits!

The "Grave Dancer"

Another individual you may never have heard of is Sam Zell. The Chicago-based billionaire may be best known, by the public, for buying the Tribune Company and watching his newspaper investment head straight into bankruptcy. It was a purchase Sam admitted was a mistake.

But in reality that investment, which was small print for Sam Zell, may have made headlines, but it was just a very small sidebar story to the investment history of a man whom Wall Street has nicknamed "the grave dancer."

Sam, whom I consider to be among the greatest investors of all time, an engaging interview subject, a friend, and something of a mentor to me, is not terribly fond of the moniker given to him by the financial press.

He was called the "grave dancer" for having a vulturelike eye for spotting companies considered clinically dead by his colleagues, buying them, and reaping enormous profits when he helped revive them and return them to profitability.

Sam's specialty is real estate. At one time, Sam was both the largest commercial real estate landlord in the country and the largest residential real estate owner as well, through both his Equity Office Properties and his Equity Residential businesses.

Sam is not only expert at buying distressed investments at the bottom of a market cycle, he is also extraordinary at identifying market tops.

In 2007, he sold all of his commercial properties for a staggering $39 billion to the Blackstone Group, one of the biggest private-equity firms in the country. At the time it was the largest private-equity transaction in U.S. history. Only six months prior, Sam had told me privately that he was reluctant to sell the office properties because he couldn't find anywhere else to invest the money that would offer similar, excess rates of return.

But a few months after our chat, Sam, who is, in his own words, plagued by his knowledge of the numbers, saw that commercial real estate was getting quite "toppy" and sold the whole thing in one large chunk.

I appeared on CNBC the day the deal was announced, and was asked who, I thought, got the better of that trade. Without hesitation, I said there were only two words that viewers needed to know, "Sam sold."

While Blackstone instantly resold many of the properties at a profit, Sam's sale of Equity Office Properties marked the peak of the commercial real estate market.

Since then, commercial real estate values have plunged, along with office rents. Office vacancies and falling rents now pose a $1.3 trillion problem for the banking industry, as commercial mortgages go sour.

As for Sam, he stated in an interview in May 2009 that the residential real estate market may be finding "equilibrium." Should the "grave dancer" start buying plots of residential real estate, you should be doing the same!

Gross Profits

For the individual investor, Bill Gross may very well be the most recognizable name in this chapter. As the founder and co-chief executive officer of PIMCO (the Pacific Investment Management Company, now owned by Germany's insurance giant Allianz), Gross is a uniquely familiar face to investors and CNBC viewers everywhere.

Known as the "Bond King," Gross oversees the management of about $800 billion in assets, up from the $12 million

PIMCO started with in 1971. The PIMCO Total Return Fund, managed by Gross, is the largest bond fund anywhere, with over $150 billion in assets.

I've known Bill since the 1980s, and throughout my association with him, I have found him to be among the most astute market analysts, economic historians, and money managers of any kind. He is most often well ahead of the pack when it comes to identifying major market trends and has done his level best to help his clients profit from his foresight.

In his career as a bond fund manager, Gross has racked up annualized gains of over 10 percent per year, an astounding feat, since *his* bond-fund returns are equal to the long-run returns on stocks. Bonds typically return 4 percent per year, less than half the return on equities. That makes Gross's profits the best in the bond business.

While Gross is more of a traditional institutional investor than Paulson or Zell, he is also uniquely positioned to offer guidance to individual investors seeking to boost their returns during this stressful market environment.

Gross's firm, PIMCO, has been advising the federal government on how to go about fixing the financial system, how banks should dispose of so-called toxic assets, and how to restore growth to an economy deep in recession. This is nothing new. Like many savvy and important market participants, Bill is in frequent contact with economic policy makers who prize his views on the economy.

Speaking of prizes, Bill's investment letters have long received the highest accolades from his peers, who rate the quality of the insights he puts in print. They have been both prescient and profitable for those who took the time to read them.

Gross has repeatedly said that it is wise to put your money where Uncle Sam does. Whether that means buying mortgage securities, FDIC-backed bank bonds, Fannie Mae or Freddie Mac securities, or other credit investments, Gross says following our leaders is the safest way to make money in the current environment.

Fortunately, you can profit from Bill's advice and his expertise simultaneously. Later in the book, I'll show how mutual fund investments (some run by PIMCO) will get you into distressed assets, whether in mortgages, corporate debt, undervalued municipal paper, or "toxic assets" soon to be sold off by the nation's biggest banks.

The Oracle of Omaha

Among the investors I have named, Warren Buffett is, by far, the most famous of this group, from Main Street to Wall Street. The so-called Oracle of Omaha has spent a lifetime buying undervalued companies with great brand names or franchises and, in the process, has become one of the richest people in the world—second richest, according to *Forbes* magazine, March

2009. (There may be those who are richer than Mexico's Carlos Slim Helú, Microsoft's Bill Gates, or Berkshire Hathaway's Buffett, but for a variety of reasons, from privacy to piracy, *their* names don't end up on the Forbes 400!)

Buffett's annual meetings and shareholder letters are the stuff of Wall Street legend. His observations on the markets and his bits of wit and wisdom have become widely quoted.

Buffett studied under the great Benjamin Graham, the father of value investing. Value investors seek to buy a dollar's worth of value, or earnings power, for fifty cents in the stock market. Further, most value investors are quite adept at recognizing when Wall Street's pendulum has swung too far from greed to fear and back again. As a consequence, they tend to recognize opportunities and risks earlier than most investors, based on a highly disciplined approach to valuing assets.

In Buffett's case, he is famous for never having been burned in the technology craze; buying very cheap physical assets in the energy sector after the Enron bubble burst; and buying shares of financial firms, such as Goldman Sachs and Wells Fargo, when everyone else was selling them during the most recent crisis. He typically profits handsomely from nearly every investment he makes.

While not infallible, Buffett knows value when he sees it and has built a $35 billion fortune for himself, identifying tops and bottoms in major market trends.

The fact that he was a touch early in buying beaten-down

banks and brokerages does not diminish the fact that those investments, spurned by nearly everyone in early 2009, are beginning to pay handsome rewards as we approach 2010.

One of the most interesting things about Warren Buffett is that he rarely, if ever, spouts conventional wisdom. Like the other investors I named before, Buffett swims against the tide, calmly buying when others are frantically selling, and disposing of assets when investors are in a rush to buy.

Buffett likes bargains. What is fascinating and often mentioned about the individual investor is that he or she would rather buy and sell higher, than buy low and sell high. Most individuals know bargains among consumer products but rarely recognize them among investment opportunities.

After the Enron energy-sector bubble burst, Buffett was among the few to buy oil and gas pipelines from the defunct company, and subsequently made a fortune riding the energy wave in the years that immediately followed.

Like any great long-term investor, Buffett buys what other people want least, assuming the financials support his thesis, and sells what people want most. It's the philosophy behind what the British like to call "buying cheap and selling dear."

This is a time when it pays to behave like Paulson, Zell, Gross, and Buffett, buying when the crowd is running away and selling when the madding crowd starts rushing in.

You may get in and out early among emerging trends, but

you'll rarely be trapped in overvalued asset classes, nor will you likely miss the opportunity to buy assets on the cheap.

And, now is the time to buy many assets on the cheap, as the following chapters will show.

Vulture vs. Value

I just want to quickly distinguish between the types of investing I am recommending in this book: vulture versus value.

Vulture investors, like Sam Zell, look for truly bombed-out investments that are selling at only pennies on the dollar. Those assets can either be restored to health, to realize a profit, or liquidated, to provide an excess return on the original investment.

Value investors, like Warren Buffett, meanwhile seek opportunities to buy companies at a discount to key metrics, such as book value, cash flow, or some other measure of valuation.

They are not out to liquidate a company's assets, typically, though they may apply pressure to a company's management to take steps to improve the operations of the firm and, by extension, greatly enhance the company's stock price or the price of another, related security.

These are different disciplines, but both apply to the work we'll be doing here.

Some opportunities that exist today are for the vultures, while others are pure value plays.

There are various types of stocks, bonds, and real estate investments (whether the real estate is the actual property or a security based on an underlying property or mortgage) that we will examine, many of which are selling at disaster prices. These are more akin to vulture-style opportunities in the market.

There are also beaten-down investments in the same category that are not having near-death experiences, which will be more value oriented.

In either case, the opportunities to make money are supported by government efforts to stabilize a wide variety of markets, from residential real estate to mortgage-backed securities, and from bank stocks to many kinds of bonds.

The government-led effort to save the economy is the key to the proposition of this book, that Washington's efforts to "reflate" the economy will also enable you to "reflate" your portfolio.

There are times when bells ring on Wall Street, signaling a unique opportunity to take advantage of Uncle Sam's help. It may come in the form of a dramatic drop in interest rates, government support programs, or assistance to buy both old and new assets.

Fortunately for us, all of the above are true, and hold the key to your investment success over the next several years.

The only work left to be done is identifying the opportunity that suits you best, from buying your first home to buying someone else's second-lien mortgage.

A common characteristic among all these investors is that they tend to be early in spotting trends. Once they spot trends, they act. They don't wait for others to recognize what is obvious to them. By the time everyone recognizes a trend, it's time to get out.

Having said that, I believe it is still very early in this distressed investing cycle, in which all kinds of assets, from real estate to stocks to bonds, will recover from the subterranean levels of this near-depressionary environment.

But the question for you is, will you follow these market leaders and hop off the sidelines and into the game?

Not all investments are made for everyone. In this book I hope to show you multiple ways in which to make money, each of which may meet your specific needs, risk tolerance, or financial ability.

The real work begins now.

Resource Guide

There are limitless resources these days to help you research investment opportunities. However, I have my favorites to help find bargains in stocks, bonds, and/or real estate.

I mention several sites throughout the book, but in the interest of consolidating the sites and sources that can later serve as a reference guide, I will list some of the most useful resources in this chapter.

Obviously, my favorite content sites include CNBC.com and TheStreet.com. The first is my employer in TV; the other a joint-venture partner in my *Market Movers* newsletter. Both sites provide superior content for business news and stock-market research, and both provide unique forums on specific sectors of the economy and the markets.

Beyond that, your daily news reading regimen, all of which can be done online, should include, without fail, the following:

- *The Wall Street Journal*
- *The Financial Times*
- *The New York Times*
- *The Washington Post*
- The *Drudge Report* (an aggregated look at stories you may have missed elsewhere)

This is a quick way to get up to speed on the day's news and important headlines before you begin your research.

The specific sites I use to dig deeper into my investment prospects, beyond CNBC and TheStreet, include TD Ameritrade, the stock-trading platform I use to handle my equity account.

As I illustrate later in the book, you can find stock, bond, and mutual-fund information, including both fundamental and technical analyses of various investments; screens that allow you to build watch lists that will alert you when a particular investment reaches a price you are willing to pay; and other tools that make your investing life easier and more efficient.

Research services such as Morningstar offer deep dives into stock, bond, domestic equity, emerging-market, and other types of mutual funds, while also analyzing real estate investment trusts (REITS), hedge funds, and other investment vehicles, and providing historical returns data and a rating system for top-performing investment vehicles.

A five-star rating at Morningstar is the highest accolade a fund can earn.

For real estate itself, I frequently use:

- Realtor.com
- Condo.com
- Zillow.com

To locate foreclosure opportunities, the following sites are quite interesting:

- RealtyTrac.com
- Foreclosure.com
- Gorilla.com

As I point out later in the book in "Do-It-Yourself Distressed," there are now sites that allow you to buy distressed mortgages online or as part of an online auction. They are relatively new sites and include:

- DebtX.com
- Loanmarket.com
- Bigbidder.com
- SellYourTimeShareNow.com

And, of course, all arms of the government, from the U.S. Treasury to Housing and Urban Development to the USDA, are jettisoning foreclosed and seized properties, many of which can be viewed at the Web addresses that are given on subsequent pages.

In brief, there is no shortage of resources to help you get started on rebuilding your broken nest egg, and using government resources or direct or indirect government programs to help finance and enhance the distressed investments that are in abundant supply today.

As I suggest later, I believe real estate to be the biggest bargain of all, despite the worst real estate bear market in U.S. and global history. In fact, it's because of the crash that I believe real estate represents the buying opportunity of a lifetime.

No doubt many of you are reluctant to enter or venture

back into the real estate market. But as you will see, real estate, and a variety of other investments, are extraordinarily cheap by historic standards.

It is my very strongly held point of view that our generation probably will not see another opportunity like this in our lifetime. If that notion intrigues, then, by all means, read on.

The Main Street Mind vs. the Wall Street Mind

One of the most fascinating things I have discovered by watching consumers and investors over the last twenty-five years is that they behave very differently, even though a consumer and an investor may very well be embodied in the exact same person. We all do some of both, though most Americans do more consuming than investing.

Consumer spending accounts for about 71 percent of America's GDP. That's the highest percentage on record. Fueled by easily available and overabundant credit (until recently!), Americans went on a buying binge over the last few decades, the likes of which the world has never seen.

This was true of investors, as well, in the last two decades. They snapped up any dot.com company they could find in the 1990s and any house or condo they could hunt down in the early 2000s. But that behavior was not the stuff of consumerlike bargain hunting. It was born of the notion that

31

one could buy high, and sell higher. (That's what economists describe as "the greater fool theory"!)

Clearly, there is an amazing Jekyll-and-Hyde–like split between our consuming selves and our investing selves. One is timid and often paralyzed by fear. The other is fearless and aggressive.

Unfortunately for us, Dr. Jekyll is the investor and Mr. Hyde is the consumer!

The "consumer inside" will use any and all means necessary to make anything from the most intelligent to the most imprudent purchases possible, reading *Consumer Reports* or navigating the World Wide Web in search of a deal.

Mutual fund legend Peter Lynch once observed that individuals will spend infinitely more time researching the purchase of a refrigerator or a DVD player (when he said it, it was a VCR!) than researching an investment into which they dedicate their life savings.

That was true during the mutual fund mania of the 1990s, and it was true again during the mortgage mania of more recent vintage. How many of us bothered to read the details of our mortgages, whether they were simple fixed-rate agreements or more complicated adjustable, partial interest-only mortgages, which ultimately surprised us with mushrooming monthly payments after a two- or three-year grace period?

How ironic is it that a consumer will bravely hunt down any bargain, wait patiently in line for hours at garage, clearance, holiday, or liquidation sales to get 10, 25, or 50 percent off? He or she will haggle with a car salesman like a medieval merchant at a bazaar to wring the last penny out of a car purchase, or become a virtual techno-wizard to Google the best buys among the latest available gadgetry.

Meanwhile, the "average investor inside" does just the opposite, fleeing from the frequent downward spirals in the financial markets, despite the values created in stock-market sell-offs. He or she shies away from bargains on Wall Street while searching for sales on Main Street.

Investors will bury their heads in the sand when quarterly statements come and pretend that price "adjustments" in markets are always "panicky" problems, not opportunities to take advantage of.

It has taken me countless years to reverse this type of psychology in myself. My dual personality, comprised of two-thirds consumer and one-third "average investor," is still alive and well, but the pro is beginning to take over.

I now recognize that no matter how serious the market decline is, or how scary the stock market, or any market, may feel when it's in free fall, the "professional investor" inside me should take over.

Or, more precisely, I need to act like a professional investor who, ironically, is very much like the average consumer, someone who always knows a bargain when he or she sees one.

Right now, America is literally on sale. Whether it's

foreclosed residential real estate or falling office rent, whether it's a beaten-down financial stock or a mangled municipal bond, whether it's a junkier junk bond or a high-quality piece of art, prices have come crashing down in the last two years and all of these things are now available at prices you can afford.

The financial crisis we have just experienced has been described by many, including former Federal Reserve chairman Alan Greenspan, as a "once-in-a-century" event. As a consumer/investor, you can think of this not as a twenty-first-century event, but as a "Century 21" event. (For those of you not in the New York metropolitan area, Century 21 is a department store that sells brand-name merchandise at a discount.)

These are the types of bargains the consumer would die for, if they were men's or women's outfits, shoes, refrigerators, computers, iPods, or flat-screen TVs! If you saw a Web site like SmartBargains.com for investments, you'd go wild! Seventy-eight percent off brand-name merchandise? With free shipping?

But those bargains do exist! A colleague of mine picked up an $80,000, twenty-six-foot, full-bedroom, full-bath RV for $30,000. Everyone knows *that's* a deal. But does he or she recognize brand-name investments that are selling at equally steep discount prices?

World markets have been marked down by 30 to 70 percent from the bull market peak in 2007 to the bear market trough of 2009!

And while many asset classes rallied sharply in the first half of 2009, they remain 40 to 50 percent below their all-time highs.

In other words, it continues to look a lot like Christmas on Wall Street, everywhere you go in the investing world, even though the "Grinch" has stolen the gifts from many of our neighbors and friends.

It may not feel good to go out shopping right now, but it's the right thing to do if your "inner consumer" can convince your "inner investor" to align their behavior.

I used to work in retail when I was in college, helping to pay my own way. I worked in a vitamin store in L.A.'s San Fernando Valley. Inside the mall where I worked, I marveled at how people lined up inside and outside our store when we sold packages of heavily discounted vitamins. You wouldn't believe how long the lines were when we sold a bottle of synthetic vitamin E for $2.99!

Quite frequently there would be mall-wide sales events. There would be a mad rush at the Broadway, a now-bankrupt West Coast retailer, which would pile purses on a table, and customers would literally trample one another to buy a designer handbag for 25 percent off! That's how we act on Main Street.

Ironically, on Wall Street we trample one another to buy the goods that are rising in price and flee the building when prices are falling!

Even when prices have *stopped* falling, we don't have the nerve to buy financial assets at a discount. Instead, we wait for others to validate our sublimated urges, and the market's trend, by watching them bid prices up. It is typically then, and only then, that we start buying again. And sometimes by then it may just be too late to make any money.

This is the conundrum that Dr. Jekyll and Mr. Hyde face in the financial markets. Interestingly, the time to be Dr. Jekyll, the timid and fearful one, is when everyone else is Mr. Hyde, and vice versa.

Look around you today. Nearly everyone is frightened to death by what is going on in the economy and in the markets. And given recent experience, it is understandable. But from an investor's viewpoint, it also doesn't matter.

What matters is what we do now! I can't stress enough that the past has passed. I am not suggesting that we pretend it didn't happen or ignore any warning signs that things could deteriorate again. But I also do not think it wise or prudent for individuals to let Dr. Jekyll inhabit their bodies for too long. You can't run, but at this moment in time, you should Hyde!

Risk and Reward

I understand that the tone of this book can sound a little cavalier to the individual who is fearful of losing his or her job, home, savings, or standing in the community. I don't mean it to be so.

I also do not mean to suggest that investing in distressed assets such as real estate, stocks, high-yield bonds, or even government-backed bonds is entirely without risk. It is not.

Every investment is fraught with risk, although the riskiest time to invest, to be quite honest, is when investors are most complacent about the dangers of investing. That was true two years ago, when the Dow was at 14,000 and when houses were selling like hotcakes.

Still, we are not out of the woods when it comes to investing, and I don't want to mislead you in any way that suggests we are. Before we go on, I believe it is my responsibility to outline the risks that you will be taking if you get back into the markets, whether it's real estate, stocks, or bonds.

First and foremost—despite the so-called green shoots springing up in the economy, suggesting that the dead of winter has passed in this "Great Recession"—this is by no means a certainty, as it is with the four seasons.

It is true that the worst appears to be behind us. That is the assessment of everyone from President Obama to Fed chairman Ben Bernanke to Treasury secretary Tim Geithner to a wide variety of economists and famous professional investors and businesspeople.

However, many of them thought the same thing in the

spring of 2007, after the first sub-prime scare, and that proved to be just the beginning of the recession, not the end.

Admittedly, two years later, it's clear that a lot has gone wrong and it is highly unlikely that we will witness a repeat of that dismal performance in the markets or the economy.

Still, the economy and the markets face numerous headwinds that could derail an economic and market recovery or, worse, could push us deeper into a recession before we ever fully recover.

Among the concerns I have, the following appear most threatening:

1. The ballooning budget deficit, estimated to be nearly $1.6 trillion in fiscal year 2009, will drive up interest rates and, more important, mortgage rates, aborting any recovery before it even begins. (Indeed, by late spring, interest rates had climbed noticeably, pushing up mortgage rates close to 6 percent and slowing down the apparent stabilization and expected improvement in housing.)

2. Despite the record deficits and historic spending programs being used by the Obama administration to stimulate the economy, they still may not be sufficiently large, or sufficiently effective, to return the economy to a healthy rate of growth.

3. Oil and gasoline prices may continue to rise, sapping consumers of their buying power and sending us back into

recession. (A combination of numbers 1, 2, and 3 would be lethal.)

4. Banks could suffer another round of staggering and potentially perilous losses from rising credit-card defaults and $1.3 trillion worth of souring commercial real estate loans. None of those things has yet been fully factored into bank-stock prices and their profit outlooks, the financial markets, or the economy as a whole.

5. As I write this, I also worry about several of the world's "hot spots":

- North Korea is threatening to "weaponize" its nuclear materials and ready itself for war with South Korea and the West.

- Iran's president, Mahmoud Ahmadinejad, has been declared the winner in a contested presidential election, while his chief rival is also claiming victory. Another Iranian revolution could drive oil prices to unheard-of levels and destabilize both global politics and the global economy. It also could end up being a huge positive for the global economy if the uprisings lead to an overthrow of the Muslim clerics in charge and bring Iran into the family of nations.

- In a televised interview on July 5, 2009 Vice President Joe Biden said Israel has the right to deal with Iran however it sees fit, despite Washington's point of view. On the same day, published reports said Saudi Arabia would ignore Israeli planes flying over its airspace if they were en route to blowing up Iran's nuclear facilities!

- The Taliban and the Pakistani government are battling for control of Pakistan and Islamabad's nuclear arsenal.

An eruption in any of the world's "hot spots," from those mentioned here to Venezuela to Nigeria, also could deal a critical setback to a global rebound.

Having reviewed most of what could go wrong in the immediate future—and there are other unforeseen risks—we can begin to move forward now, slightly more comfortable and confident that, absent an unexpected setback, it is still the time to reposition our portfolios for the coming rebound in distressed assets, across many asset classes.

Cash Is Trash!

The "Great Recession" has produced some interesting phenomena, not the least of which is a rapidly rising savings rate in the United States. Better known as a nation of spendthrifts than savers, the United States now sports its highest savings rate since 1993, fluctuating between 5 and 7 percent, and the highest total dollar amount, $768 billion, since 1959!

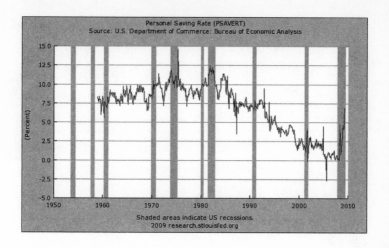

Granted, it was, at least partly, boosted by onetime govern-ment stimulus checks, but it's still "a good thing," as Martha Stewart would say.

The savings rate in the United States has been, effectively, below 1 percent since the beginning of 2005, and sometimes even below zero.

The replenishment of personal savings is necessary to restore the consumer, and the economy, to health, but it is also a double-edged sword. The more consumers save, the less they buy, keeping the economy from accelerating toward more normal levels of growth.

But given the historically high debt levels carried by consumers in recent years, the rising savings rate helps households repair their balance sheets, if you will, and will eventually pay for the pent-up demand that has kept them from buying homes, cars, and other goods and services.

The savings can, as I indicated, also be used to pay down debt, particularly costly credit-card debt, which is a major tax on the consumer's ability to continue spending.

Even more important, I believe that the higher savings rate could and should be used by individuals to take advantage of the investment opportunities before them today.

Short-term Treasuries are paying a fraction of 1 percent. The most generous bank CDs are paying low single-digit rates of return. Investors are being punished, not intentionally, by being too risk averse!

The time to be risk averse is when everyone else is taking too many risks. Now everyone is frightened and still hoarding cash, despite signs that markets are functioning better and that riskier assets are providing much more enticing returns than cash.

This is not the time to keep your money under your mattress! That day has passed. The buildup in your savings account should first and foremost go toward paying down high-cost debt, but after that, it is time to sink money into a house, beaten-down stocks and bonds, or any other asset class that can help you rebuild your wealth.

This is not the time to be left behind. The train may be leaving the station, but there is still plenty of time to catch it, particularly for patient money that knows a bargain when it sees one.

Jack Ablin, the chief market strategist at Chicago-based Harris Private Bank, a unit of Harris Trust, put out a mid-2009 report noting that, at the time of his writing, cash appeared to be king. The numbers he described in his report show just how shell-shocked investors were at this low point of the real estate/credit/stock market crash.

Assets of money-market mutual funds swelled to 65 percent of the stock market's total value! That was a record. Never before had individuals hoarded so much cash at one time. However, as you'll see from Ablin's note below, there is enough of your cash on the sidelines to power a stock market rally for the next two years!

CURRENT MARKET UPDATE

Liquidity is the ingredient that fuels spending and investment. If you don't have it, you can't spend it. Americans, in the aftermath of the financial market meltdown, have salted away piles of cash. Nearly half the value of the U.S. stock market is parked on the sidelines in short-term investments. As long as the ranks of stock market sufferers haven't written off equities completely, this enormous stockpile of scratch could power the stock market's next leg up. History has shown that whenever cash on the sidelines creeps over 25 percent of the capitalization of the S&P 500, the market tends to rally over the twenty-four months, as money filters

43

into the market. Today's liquidity level is a bullish indicator for stocks for the next two years.

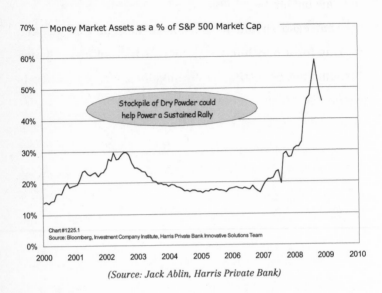

(Source: Jack Ablin, Harris Private Bank)

From March to June of 2009, that cash pile had fallen to 45 percent . . . money moved back into equity mutual funds as the market rallied nearly 40 percent from March 9 to June 1, 2009.

Ablin argues that cash in money-market mutual funds, which totaled $3.5 trillion as of June 2009, may sit on the sidelines for quite some time if investors remain gun-shy, despite the biggest three-month rally in stocks since 1933. If investors jump off the sidelines and pour their money back into the market . . . watch out above! (The comparison to 1933 is not a reassuring one to you, I'm sure. But as I mentioned

44

earlier, if you bought stocks in 1932, or 1933 for that matter, the market never retouched the lows hit at the market's penultimate bottom.)

That cash should be burning a hole in your pocket, looking for a new home, or other distressed investments. It should not be resting on the sidelines, where it is barely earning a return!

I am not suggesting we can turn your cash into instant riches, but I am telling you that "cash is trash," and it should be working for you rather than sitting idle, giving someone other than you the opportunity to use it!

4

WALL STREET IN DISTRESS

WALL STREET SUFFERED ITS ROUGHEST RIDE IN DECADES OVER the last year and a half, dropping like a stone almost every month, from its all-time high in 2007 to its early-2009 lows.

It was one of the most savage and unrelenting bear markets on Wall Street that we've seen in post–World War II history. Indeed, this financial crisis has no modern equal.

Federal Reserve chairman Ben Bernanke acknowledged in his semiannual report to Congress on July 22, 2009, that this most recent crisis may very well be the worst in economic history! I've met with Chairman Bernanke in the past, and he is not one given to fits of hyperbole just to make a point. You can be sure that if he said it, he meant it.

From its peak of over 14,000 on October 9, 2007, the Dow Jones Industrial Average plunged to a low of about 6,600 on March 9, 2009, a staggering 53 percent decline in only 18 months.

The chart below tells the story in graphic detail. Some $10 trillion in stock-market values were lost, peak to trough. That's only a couple trillion dollars less than the total output of the nation's economy, or GDP!

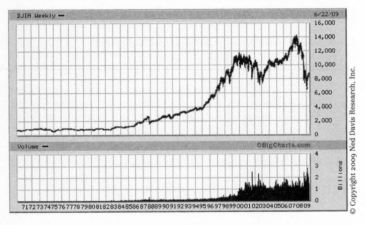

(Source: BigCharts.com)

The loss of wealth has been a critical factor in weakening the U.S. economy, especially when coupled with the $3 trillion in lost real estate values. That one-two punch in the pocketbook has knocked consumers and investors back on their heels, creating a "negative wealth effect," the likes of which we have not seen since our grandparents were teenagers.

48

Indeed, the mauling of Wall Street by this ferocious bear has only one modern precedent, and it resides in the late 1920s and early 1930s.

While there are marked differences between the crash and "Great Recession" that we are experiencing today and the crash and the Great Depression, which began eighty years ago, there are some unfortunate similarities as well.

Both economic crises began with a bust in real estate and stock-market values. Both spilled over to the general economy with alarming speed, causing a deep contraction in economic growth, not just at home, but all around the world.

The differences between this Great Recession and the Great Depression, however, are equally stark. A research paper published by Paul Swartz of the Council on Foreign Relations (CFR, June 5, 2009, www.cfr.org) shows how industrial production, unemployment, and trade fared far more poorly in the Depression than they are faring in today's recession.

Swartz also shows how deflation, or falling prices, occurred much more quickly in the 1930s than today.

The government efforts to revive the markets and stimulate the economy, which are unparalleled in economic history and were only barely attempted in the 1930s, have, as I write, borne some fruit. Indeed, they are the *very reason* I am writing this book. To date, they have not cemented a recovery, for the markets or for the economy, though I expect that they will, just as this book is being released.

Unfortunately for us, however, there are two areas of concern that are quite similar to the problems experienced some eighty years ago.

First, global trade is collapsing just as quickly as it did in the 1930s, despite the absence of trade protectionism that wrecked the world trading system during the Depression.

Equally, or maybe even more unfortunate, as Swartz clearly illustrates, stock prices are tracing out the exact same pattern today as they did during and following the 1929 crash, despite the more forceful economic policies that have been put in place (mentioned above). While that frightening little tidbit should make you a bit nervous, in some ways it should excite you as well. It means that we are as close as ever to a once-in-a-generation buying opportunity in the stock market, just as we are in real estate and in other asset classes as well.

In an interview on CNBC, on June 24, 2009, legendary investor Warren Buffett said that stocks are among the best investments to make over the next ten years. Sitting in cash, he said, will actually lose you money if inflation accelerates, which he believes will happen.

The ten-year time frame provides for an interesting comparison. In the 1970s, the last great bear market between the 1930s and today, the market behaved somewhat similarly.

Is this the type of pattern we might expect in stocks after a 50 percent plunge, like the 43 percent decline the market suffered from the start of 1973 to the end of 1974?

I happen to respectfully disagree with Buffett on the inflation issue in the near term, but later in the book I will explain how to hedge your inflation risk with a special type of bond, while also taking advantage of the opportunities being discussed here.

I have been a buyer of stocks since March 2009, but I am not doing so indiscriminately, nor do I recommend that anyone adopt that approach.

There are some critical concerns that you should be aware of before you go out and buy any and all stocks, without taking into account the several factors that cause you short-term trading pain while you wait for your long-term investing gains to materialize.

- **First, the 40 percent rally in stock prices from the March 9, 2009, low is eerily similar to a 50 percent rally traced out in 1930, after the market's first big decline took place.**

Such a "bear-market rally"—some call it a "sucker's rally"—roars very much like a bull market and tempts traders and investors back onto Wall Street with its speed and ferocity.

Afraid to miss the big move, investors get back in but fail to get out before the bear comes out of his cave again. These bear-market rallies can be extremely deceiving, and there is no guarantee that the Dow will not dive below its March 9, 2009, low.

The same was true after the 1929 crash. Despite the

intervening rally in 1930, stocks resumed a furious decline in the next two years.

From late 1930 to mid-1932, the Dow plunged again, this time shedding an even greater amount and closing at a thirty-six-year low of 41.22 on July 8, 1932. By the time the granddaddy of all bear markets was done, the Dow had lost 89.9 percent of its value. It would not reach its 1929 high of 381 again until 1954!

That's the bad news. The good news is that unless you bought all of your stock holdings in 1929, or in 2007, there were opportunities to reinvest at lower prices and let the market move higher, over the course of time.

- **Second, a major risk facing stock-market investors today is that policy makers might err in their efforts to revive the economy and begin withdrawing their stimulus measures too quickly, before the markets regain their footing and before the economy is on terra firma.**

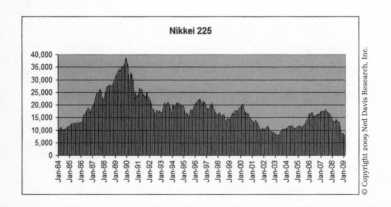

Japan made that mistake on numerous occasions after *its* financial markets crashed in the early 1990s. As a consequence of its policy mistakes, Japan's version of the Dow, the Nikkei 225, has been in a bear market for the last twenty years, and its economy has been in a recession, or worse, for at least ten of those years.

As you can see, the Nikkei hasn't even come close to regaining its all-time high of twenty years ago, thanks to very poor economic planning on the part of the Japanese government

There has been talk throughout much of 2009 about how policy makers, specifically the Federal Reserve, will unwind the trillions of dollars in various economic stimulus efforts, market-support programs, and other backstops put in place over the last fifteen months or so to avoid overstimulating the economy and creating inflation, or even worse, hyperinflation.

Such concerns are ill founded. The biggest risk facing Wall Street and Main Street is not the unintended inflationary consequences of these policies but the disastrous consequences, as we have seen before, of ending the programs too soon.

It is something that keeps me awake at night as I examine my own portfolio, and it is a danger I have spoken and written about extensively in recent months.

- **Finally, the other risks to a sustained and sustainable**

rebound in the markets and in the economy center on political and geopolitical risk. Will the Obama administration and Congress, in an effort to correct the excesses of recent years, overregulate specific industries, such as banking and brokerage, health care and pharmaceuticals?

Will they raise taxes too much, in order to to reduce the ballooning budget deficit and to offset the enormous costs of new government programs, killing the positive effects of middle-class tax reductions or other efforts to revive economic growth?

Will some world event shatter investor and consumer confidence, already severely shaken by market and economic turmoil over the course of the last two years?

The answer to the latter question, of course, is always unknown. Global geopolitical events are always unpredictable and cannot necessarily be controlled or offset by economic policies.

The political concerns are, however, likely overblown, since President Obama appears to be a compromiser who would rather stand at the presidential podium for eight years than stand on principle for four.

Those are the risks that need to be considered before putting your hard-earned money back to work on Wall Street.

It is my belief that no matter what scenario you paint, the time to buy stocks is now. It will require courage, patience, and discipline. But given that the declines in many stocks have far exceeded the 50 percent plunge in

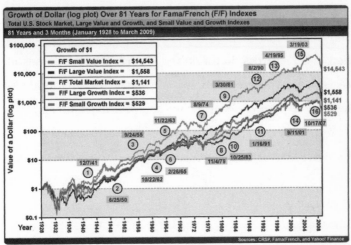

Growth of Dollar (log plot) Over 81 Years for Fama/French (F/F) Indexes
Total U.S. Stock Market, Large Value and Growth, and Small Value and Growth Indexes
81 Years and 3 Months (January 1928 to March 2009)

Growth of $1
- F/F Small Value Index = $14,543
- F/F Large Value Index = $1,558
- F/F Total Market Index = $1,141
- F/F Large Growth Index = $536
- F/F Small Growth Index = $529

Sources: CRSP, Fama/French, and Yahoo! Finance

Market Turmoil and the Dow Jones Industrial Average

	Date	Event	First Trading Session Response to Event				Subsequent Market Behavior		
			DJIA Close Previous Day	DJIA Close	DJIA Change	DJIA % Change	One Month Change	Six Months Change	One Year Change
1	12/7/41	Japan Attacks Pearl Harbor, Hawaii	115.90	112.52	-3.38	-2.92%	-0.86%	-6.19%	2.88%
2	6/25/50	North Korea Invades South Korea	224.35	213.91	-10.44	-4.65%	-4.71%	9.49%	14.67%
3	9/24/55	President Eisenhower Heart Attack	487.45	455.56	-31.89	-6.54%	1.15%	12.62%	7.06%
4	10/22/62	Cuban Missle Crisis	573.29	568.60	-4.69	-0.82%	13.41%	25.05%	31.41%
5	11/23/63	President Kennedy Assassinated	732.65	711.49	-21.16	-2.89%	6.58%	15.37%	25.19%
6	2/26/65	Vietnam Conflict	899.9	903.48	3.58	0.40%	-1.31%	-0.81%	5.37%
7	8/9/74	President Nixon Resigns	784.89	777.30	-7.59	-0.97%	-14.71%	-8.87%	5.98%
8	11/4/79	Iran Hostage Crisis	818.94	812.63	-6.31	-0.77%	1.51%	0.45%	17.29%
9	3/30/81	President Reagan Shot	994.78	992.16	-2.62	-0.26%	0.56%	-14.33%	-16.90%
10	10/25/83	Crisis in Grenada	1248.98	1252.44	3.46	0.28%	2.00%	-7.10%	-3.31%
11	8/2/90	Iraq Invades Kuwait	2899.26	2864.60	-34.66	-1.20%	-8.74%	-3.22%	4.95%
12	1/16/91	US Launches Bombing Attack on Iraq	2490.59	2508.91	18.32	0.74%	16.87%	18.93%	28.53%
13	4/19/95	Oklahoma Bombing	4179.13	4207.49	28.36	0.68%	3.18%	14.14%	31.56%
14	9/11/01	World Trade Center Towers Destroyed	9605.51	8920.70	-684.81	-7.13%	3.50%	18.58%	-7.99%
15	3/19/03	Operation Iraqi Freedom	8194.23	8265.45	71.22	0.87%	0.77%	16.69%	23.24%
16	10/17/07	Bursting of Housing Bubble	13912.94	13892.54	20.40	0.15%	6.72%	13.82%	36.28%

Sources: djindexes.com and Yahoo! Finance

the major averages, the "average" stock is far cheaper than the market as a whole and represents a historic buying opportunity for those with both time *and* money.

The hard evidence for that is clear. Look at the historical graph and companion chart on page 55, highlighting major news events that occurred as the market rebounded from the 1932 lows. A lot of bad things happened, but the market climbed that proverbial "wall of worry."

These graphics, from Index Funds Advisors, say more than mere words can convey.

Time and Money

Buying and holding stocks is a bit different from investing in real estate. If you're wrong on the direction of real estate, you still have a place to live and some nice tax breaks, assuming you can afford to stay in your home and make the payments.

If you (or I) happen to be wrong on the direction of stocks, however, there is the possibility of incurring an immediate loss of capital and household wealth. Oh, and as a result, you might not have a place to live as a result, either.

While I happen to believe that current stock prices represent a historic buying opportunity, you will need to be patient and disciplined. It is very likely that, despite my belief that five years from now the stocks I like will be significantly higher than they are today, they will also swing wildly between now and then.

I will buy them on dips and occasionally take some protective measures to lock in gains along the way. But my fundamental thesis is this: We have just been through the steepest decline in stocks since the 1929–1932 period.

And unless we repeat the 1930s, which I believe to be unlikely as I have stated many times, stocks are a bargain; particularly those hit the hardest, such as financials, home builders, insurers, and big industrial companies. (I'll be more explicit about stock selection later in this chapter.)

You will probably need a strong stomach to invest in stocks. I expect that volatility will spike from time to time, as Wall Street worries that a full economic recovery may not take hold, or that government actions may hold back growth—but stock market investing is inherently risky. It takes some degree of intestinal fortitude to "place your bets and take your chances."

But with the market having fallen 53 percent, peak to trough, you don't need to catch the bottom exactly, you just need to catch it somewhere, and commit a regular amount of capital to the market as part of a disciplined, long-term approach to investing on Wall Street.

I say long-term because I believe, as stated, that patience will be required. I don't believe that individuals with short time horizons should be in this market, because, quite frankly, it can do absolutely anything over the next five years.

The market, rather than specific sectors that I will discuss later, has arguably been in a bear phase since 2000, or before. Some market analysts say the market's "momentum" peak was in 1998, at the height of the dot.com frenzy.

Since 1998, the S&P 500 has essentially gone nowhere; actually, it's gone down, despite the great sound and fury since a great bull market began on October 11, 1990. If an investor had the foresight to understand the nature of the market mania at the time, and some folks I know did, they would have sold stocks in 1998 and bought U.S. Treasury Bonds.

Such a move would have captured all the profits from the bull market that lasted from 1990 to 2000 and enhanced them, while bonds rallied sharply in the ensuing years.

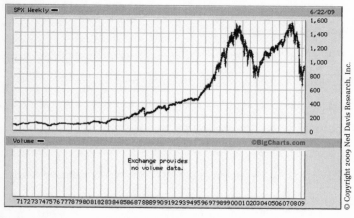

(Source: BigCharts.com)

It sounds much easier than it looks. In between two big bear markets was a historic rally. In late 2002, another big buying opportunity emerged in stocks, in the wake of the dot.com bubble bursting on Wall Street and the terror attacks of 9/11.

The S&P 500 doubled from the 2002 low to the 2007 high.

All of it, some say, was just a rally in a bear market that started in 2000, since the entire gain from 1998 to 2007 has now been given back.

A switch back into stocks in 2002 would have recouped for you the money lost from 2000 to 2002, from a market point of view. Sure—everyone says hindsight is twenty-twenty.

But some of us called for a rally in stocks, real estate, and other investments in 2002, despite warnings to the contrary. We also issued warnings in late 1999 and early 2000 about an impending crash, just as many of us did in late 2007.

That's why I am equally confident today that I can see a bottom forming in stocks.

Plus, the crash we have just endured, the second in ten years, and the second largest in eighty years, just increases the chances that we are much closer to the end of a major bear market and not the beginning of a new one.

True, some pundits who have been bearish for decades now say this is "the Big One!" and there is much more down-side to come, forecasting a drop in the Dow to 4,000 or to 400 in the S&P.

I don't know about you, but to me the chart featured on page 58 suggests "the Big One" has already come and gone!

Just for the sake of argument, let's say the "perma-bears"

are right. If you put a fixed amount of money into the market every month, a practice known as dollar-cost averaging, your cost of owning stocks during the decline would be about 25 percent lower than it is now. Your average cost would be roughly a mean average between the highest and lowest prices paid for an investment in the Dow 30 or the S&P 500 or another market index.

Over the course of the next ten to thirty years, depending on the time it takes you to reach retirement, stock prices will almost certainly be higher than they are now, or will be in the next year or two.

In the disaster scenario of the 1930s, it took twenty-five years for the Dow to regain its peak of 381, reached in September 1929.

Put in today's terms, if the "secular," or long-term, bear market started in 1998, we have fifteen years left to go of rising and falling prices before the Dow hits 14,000 again. If your average cost between now and then is 6,000, your retirement money will more than double by the time you need it.

And that's the disaster case! If, indeed, we hit the lows of this bear market on March 9, 2009, at around 6,600 on the Dow, then we are closer to 1932 than 1929, which means stocks will go up—not in a straight line, but up nonetheless—for many years to come.

This is no time to be an ostrich and pretend that the last few years have not been unkind to your wallet. They have been extremely difficult, both for your equity on Wall Street and your home equity on Main Street.

But this is also no time to fear the future. Fear is the enemy of disciplined investing, not its friend. Greed is also an enemy, but we are, for the moment, not talking about a frothy market, we are discussing a depressed one.

I can't lie to you and say that it's a sure thing you will make money in stocks. If you need your money because you're already retired, or are saving for a down payment on a house, or have other short-term obligations, putting those funds in the stock market is a terrible idea, even though I think stocks are going higher.

Putting short-term needs at risk is always a bad idea. Investing—for individuals, in particular—is a long-term game. I am not a fan of the "buy and hold" philosophy that Wall Street pushes hard when it wants your money, but I think it is a philosophy that makes more sense today than at any other time in recent memory.

The easiest and most cost-effective way to play an expected increase in stock prices is to simply "buy the market." By that I mean buying proxies for market averages—for example, exchange-traded funds (ETFs) that mirror the performance of the market's major averages, such as the Dow Industrials and the S&P 500.

You can get more specific exposure to selected areas of the stock market by using targeted investments—for example, high-tech companies in the NASDAQ 100; "small cap" stocks in the Russell 2000; international exposure through a variety of ETFs; and exposure to particular market sectors through investments in consumer staples, or semiconductors, or hard-asset plays such as real estate, oil, gold, silver, or a basket of commodities.

I would warn you to stay away from so-called leveraged ETFs, which use borrowed money to double, or triple, the returns of the market or of individual sectors. They trade very erratically and are currently being widely discussed among market observers as tools for market manipulation by speculators.

With respect to building a portfolio that gives you broad exposure to the stock market, you can easily achieve this by purchasing the Spider Trust Series 1 (SPY), an ETF that costs one-tenth the price of the S&P 500 and tracks its daily performance. There are also ETFs, as mentioned above, that track the NASDAQ 100 (QQQ) or the iShares Russell 2000 (IWM).

You also can buy many, many index funds that do the same thing. Index funds are mutual funds that track the underlying index for which they are named. The costs of index funds, like ETFs, tend to be very low and have very low investment minimums, making them affordable and tax efficient for individual investors. From Vanguard's S&P 500 Index Fund to Fidelity's Four-in-One Index Fund, there is variety of ways to be invested "in the market" without having to make specific choices about individual stocks or sectors.

To make it very simple, for a "buy and hold" strategy that

just desires market exposure, a blend of ETFs or mutual funds that capture the S&P 500, the NASDAQ 100, the Russell 2000, and the world market index, known as the MSCI EAFE index, in four equal parts is a very simple, though slightly redundant, mix that allows you to profit from the upside in U.S., and world market, rallies.

Stocks should be a large component of an investment portfolio if, again, you have at least a ten-year time horizon. There are other assets that make sense to invest in right now, which I will discuss in subsequent chapters. I also will suggest a model portfolio that divides your investing dollars among stocks, bonds, and other opportunistic investments that might maximize your gains over the next several years.

With respect to getting invested in the market, which I think is highly appropriate right now for investors with a ten-year or longer time horizon, I also reserve the right to change my mind. If storm clouds gather again, I will likely be among the first to let you know, whether on TV, radio, or in print, that I have changed my mind and want to sell my stocks until conditions feel more comfortable to me.

But the opportunities being created today in real estate, stocks, certain types of bonds, and other asset classes are, as I said, rather rare. And you rarely get the opportunity to recapture lost money.

When lost money can be found again, it's time to start looking!

Stocks to Bank On, or, the World According to TARP

Contrary to the opinions of many investors on Wall Street, I have been a big fan of the financials since I launched a pilot portfolio for a friend who runs a boutique trading firm. (You can keep track of this portfolio in my newsletter, TheStreet .com's *Market Movers* by Ron Insana.)

Company Name*	Current Quote	Initial Purchase Date**	Most Recent Trade Date
Bank of America Corporation BAC	$12.24	4/28/2009	7/9/2009
BlackRock Incorporated BLK	$184.18	7/15/2009	7/15/2009
Bristol-Myers Squibb Company BMY	$20.20	7/15/2009	7/15/2009
Citigroup Incorporated C	$2.75	4/28/2009	7/9/2009
Continental Airlines Incorporated CAL	$9.28	6/9/2009	6/9/2009
Cisco Systems Incorporated CSCO	$21.48	7/15/2009	7/15/2009
The Walt Disney Company DIS	$25.48	7/15/2009	7/15/2009
E*TRADE Financial Corporation ETFC	$1.29	6/22/2009	6/22/2009
Ford Motor Company F	$6.32	7/2/2009	7/2/2009
General Electric Company GE	$11.58	3/24/2009	7/9/2009
Huntington Bancshares Incorporated HBAN	$3.72	7/9/2009	7/9/2009
The Hartford Financial Services Group HIG	$12.16	4/9/2009	4/9/2009
Hovnanian Enterprises Inc. HOV	$2.73	3/24/2009	7/9/2009

This illustrates the portfolio as of July 22, 2009. It is illustrative of how I think an "early cycle" portfolio of stocks should be constructed in order to benefit from the economic recovery that, in my view, will disproportionately benefit interest-rate-sensitive stocks such as banks and home builders. Those groups are "overweighted" in the portfolio, while other stocks, such as asset managers and key industrials, are also prominent.

# of Shares	Cost Basis per Share	Current Value	$ Gain/Loss	% Gain/Loss
2,146	$10.19	$26,267.04	$4,398.00	20.11%
115	$177.15	$21,180.70	$808.45	3.97%
1,025	$19.58	$20,705.00	$635.50	3.17%
8,834	$2.92	$24,293.50	($1,544.04)	−5.98%
1,000	$10.00	$9,280.00	($720.00)	−7.20%
1,030	$19.33	$22,124.40	$2,214.50	11.12%
850	$23.64	$21,658.00	$1,564.00	7.78%
7,700	$1.30	$9,933.00	($77.00)	−0.77%
2,000	$5.61	$12,640.00	$1,420.00	12.66%
1,060	$10.56	$12,274.80	$1,082.00	9.67%
2,500	$3.71	$9,300.00	$25.00	0.27%
500	$10.05	$6,080.00	$1,055.00	21%
5,460	$1.71	$14,905.80	$5,553.60	59.38%

Company Name*	Current Quote	Initial Purchase Date**	Most Recent Trade Date
J.C. Penney Company Incorporated JCP	$28.97	7/15/2009	7/15/2009
JPMorgan Chase & Company JPM	$36.63	6/9/2009	7/9/2009
Lennar Corp Cl A LEN	$10.68	3/24/2009	7/9/2009
Pfizer Incorporated PFE	$16.43	7/15/2009	7/15/2009
Raymond James Financial Inc. RJF	$18.22	7/15/2009	7/15/2009
State Street Corporation STT	$47.03	7/15/2009	7/15/2009
iShares:Barc TIPS Bond TIP	$100.96	7/15/2009	7/15/2009
Toll Brothers Incorporated TOL	$17.63	3/24/2009	7/9/2009
Time Warner Incorporated TWX	$26.86	7/15/2009	7/15/2009
US Bancorp USB	$18.98	4/28/2009	7/9/2009
Verizon Communications Incorporated VZ	$30.45	7/15/2009	7/15/2009
Wells Fargo & Company WFC	$23.90	4/28/2009	7/9/2009

On August 3, 2009, I moved the portfolio to an all-cash position. I will, however, have repurchased these shares by mid-autumn, after an expected correction offers me a reentry point at slightly less expensive levels.

I believe that the most beaten-down, or distressed, stocks will be the biggest winners in the coming upturn, even despite their massive rallies from the March 9 lows.

This is a real money, not a model, portfolio. I am putting real money where my mouth is. Things could change and I

# of Shares	Cost Basis per Share	Current Value	$ Gain/Loss	% Gain/Loss
715	$28.07	$20,713.55	$643.50	3.21%
643	$34.18	$23,553.09	$1,574.35	7.16%
1,765	$9.04	$18,850.20	$2,902.70	18.20%
1,300	$14.78	$21,359.00	$2,145.00	11.16%
1,100	$18.20	$20,042.00	$22.00	0.11%
425	$47.32	$19,987.75	($123.25)	–0.61%
250	$100.36	$25,240.00	$150.00	0.60%
930	$17.42	$16,395.90	$197.90	1.22%
850	$25.33	$22,831.00	$1,300.50	6.04%
1,315	$17.91	$24,958.70	$1,412.92	6%
670	$29.50	$20,401.50	$636.50	3.22%
1,132	$21.28	$27,054.80	$2,967.66	12.32%

could be forced to restructure my holdings in the event of a major change in outlook.

But I believe that over the next two to five years, these stocks will be among the big winners as normality and sanity return to Wall Street.

Since March 2009, I have been buying bank shares for one very simple reason: After the failures of Bear Stearns, Fannie Mae and Freddie Mac, AIG, and Lehman Brothers, coupled with the forced sales of Merrill Lynch, Wachovia, and Washington Mutual, the Federal Reserve promised that no large financial institution will ever again fail on its watch.

Given the failures I just mentioned, some of which occurred because of the ineptitude of then–Treasury secretary Hank Paulson—not Fed chairman Ben Bernanke—you might think this a hollow promise indeed.

However, this promise marked a watershed moment in modern financial history. The Federal Reserve, along with a more compliant Treasury, has taken unprecedented measures to prevent another large failure that could threaten the very survival of our financial system.

But that promise has precedents from the past, which give me confidence that, once emboldened to act, the Fed will do anything and everything to bolster the banking system.

As you have heard and read, the U.S. government poured hundreds of billions of dollars into our largest banks, which were hobbled by trillions of dollars of "toxic" debt.

The Federal Reserve slashed interest rates to a never-before-seen zero percent and injected trillions of dollars into the economy, either by lending money to cash-strapped banks and brokers or by providing all sorts of guarantees to all kinds of financial institutions and products throughout different areas of the money markets.

The Bush Treasury extended $700 billion in aid to troubled banks, through the Troubled Asset Relief Program (TARP), while Congress and the Obama administration, passed nearly a trillion dollars in stimulus programs.

The FDIC insured bank debt (another opportunity I'll discuss later) and expanded the insurance coverage on bank deposits to $250,000 per account. The FDIC may extend that temporary guarantee until the middle of 2010.

When taken together, the total value of these programs approaches $13 trillion at its peak! That's equal to one year's GDP in the United States, or about a third of the entire economic output of this planet, in any given year.

Clearly, the government and the Fed did not literally spend $13 trillion, but the sum of all these different support programs is without precedent in economic history.

However, during prior banking crises—in 2001–2, in 1990–91, and in 1981–82—policy makers adopted similarly appropriate measures to bail out the banking system. In each case the effort worked, and bombed-out banking stocks rose from record lows to record highs several years later.

A great case study is Citigroup, which in 1991 teetered on the edge of insolvency, as it did again in recent months. Known then as CitiCorp, the nation's largest bank at the time was rescued by policy makers who engineered a financial fix that recapitalized all the banks, many of which nearly went bust after lending countless dollars to companies during the buyout mania of the late 1980s and early 1990s and to commercial real estate projects, many of which collapsed in value.

The accompanying chart shows that, at its depths, Citi traded just above a dollar a share, adjusted for recent stock splits. And despite the gloom-and-doom reports you are about to read, the stock was poised for a rebound of historic proportions!

Citicorp (Source: BigCharts.com)

The banking crisis sparked a panic on Wall Street in 1991 and led to articles like the following from *Time* magazine. These are must-reads if you want to understand how the pendulum swings from fear to greed, and back again, in the stock market!

PILLARS OF SAND

■

BY JOHN GREENWALD; ROBERT AJEMIAN/BOSTON,
JOHN E. GALLAGHER/NEW YORK, AND
MICHAEL RILEY/WASHINGON

Monday, Jan. 14, 1991 | Guards posted outside dozens of shuttered financial offices in Rhode Island last week were ominous portents for the troubled U.S. banking industry. Only hours after he was sworn in on New Year's Day, Governor Bruce Sundlun shut down 45 banks and credit unions to prevent a run on deposits in the wake of the collapse of the private firm that insured them. While such private insurance has become a rarity, the closings aggravated the growing anxiety about the health of the entire financial system, as the U.S., already reeling from the savings and loan debacle, sinks into a new recession.

Not since the Great Depression has the outlook for so many banks seemed so grim. The epicenter of distress is the downtrodden Northeast, where lenders in New York and New England are writing off bad loans at a furious pace. Many of the worst headaches are in New York City, which is home to seven of the 10 largest U.S. banks. Experts predict that such giants as Citicorp, the biggest U.S. banking company, Chase Manhattan (No. 3) or Chemical (No. 8) may have to merge with other large firms to survive. "There is a high chance for a major consolidation over the next one or two years," says James McDermott, who follows the industry for the Wall Street investment firm Keefe Bruyette.

Such a marriage would be just part of a broad upheaval that seems certain to reshape American banking this year. From Main Street to Wall Street to the White House, 1991 looms as a watershed for the staggering industry. Calling financial reform a top domestic priority, George Bush is preparing a proposal to free banks from regulations that bar them from crossing state lines or diversifying into new fields. Congress began to put forth its own proposals last week. Meanwhile, more than 1,000 of the nation's 12,400 commercial banks are on the government's watch list of troubled lenders, a level four times as great as during the 1981–82 recession. And the Federal Deposit Insurance Corp. expects 180 banks with total assets of $70 billion to fail this year. The cost of closing them will drain more than half the cash now in the FDIC fund that insures bank deposits, leaving a meager $4 billion on hand, unless something is done to shore up the fund.

The industry's problems have affected consumers and companies by discouraging banks from lending to any but their most creditworthy customers. The resulting credit crunch helped bring on the recession and drive up unemployment, which the government said last week reached 6.1% in December, the highest level in more than three years. Moreover, big banks have kept lending rates high to bolster sagging profits, which fell to $3.8 billion in the third quarter of 1990, down from $5.3 billion in the April-June period. Most major banks waited until last week to lower their prime rate a half-point, to 9-1/2%, even though the Federal Reserve Board had dropped its discount rate, on which the prime is largely based, two weeks earlier. Many banks are raising service charges for everything from automated-teller-machine transactions to penalties for bounced checks.

Sound remotely familiar?

(Source: Wall Street Journal)

Amid all the pessimism and fears of financial ruin, a little-known Saudi prince, His Royal Highness, Prince al Walweed bin Talal, bought an enormous stake in Citicorp for a little more than $1 per share, split-adjusted. Of the $20 billion he would be worth ten years later, roughly half his wealth came from buying Citi at bargain prices.

By 1998, as you can see on page 73, Citi increased by about thirteen times its rock-bottom price of $1.57 a share!

The same was true of bank stocks during the double-dip recession and stock market swoon from 1980 to 1982.

The double-dip recession and the international banking crisis led to press reports like the following, also from *Time* magazine, less than ten years before the crisis just mentioned!

BANKING'S CRUMBLING IMAGE

*Bad loans are causing big troubles for
America's financial industry*

■

BY CHRISTOPHER BYRON;
FREDERICK UNGEHEUER; PATRICIA DELANEY

Monday, Aug. 2, 1982 | Banks and bankers have long been considered the bedrock of American business. The sober executives dressed in dark blue and talked in hushed tones, as befitted their serious calling. Their judgment was considered Solomonic, and their financial institutions were believed to be as solid as the vaults in which their cash was stored.

No more. A surprising number of American bankers are now winning a reputation for bad loans, poor decisions and weak management. In the past six months, 22 banks have failed, and last week two major U.S. banks announced large second-quarter losses. It was the first time since World War II that one of the top ten American banks had suffered a three-month loss. New York's Chase Manhattan reported that it lost $16.1 million between April and June, while the figure for Chicago's Continental Illinois was $60.9 million during the same period.

The U.S. banking industry is by far the safest and soundest in the world. Deposits in the more than 14,000 institutions belonging to the Federal Deposit Insurance Corporation are guaranteed by the Government for up to $100,000 for each account. Since the FDIC program was established in 1934, 578 member banks have gone out of business for one reason or another, but no depositor has ever lost a penny in an insured account.

Even so, people are growing edgy about whether their deposits are still as safe as money in the bank. In recent months, newspaper reports of financial strains on local banks and savings and loan associations have brought crowds of agitated depositors into bank lobbies to withdraw their funds from cash-squeezed institutions in Miami; Hartford, Conn.; Abilene, Texas; and a number of other towns and cities. A recent survey by Burke Marketing Research Inc. of Cincinnati showed that nearly 90% of Americans questioned now have some concern about the stability of U.S. financial institutions. Only about 10% feel any real confidence in the present banking climate.

Figures released by the FDIC last week give grounds for worry. Since January the agency's problem list of state and national banks with significant financial difficulties has increased from 223 to 268, the largest number since the aftermath of the 1973–75 recession.

On Wall Street, investor jitters have sent the industry into a slide, dropping share prices of a number of big money-center banks, including Chase Manhattan and Chemical Bank, to an average of only four times earnings. That is roughly the price-earnings ratio of the severely depressed oil drilling industry.

The woes of banks have largely been caused by the combination of high interest rates and an economy that shows little sign of recovering from almost three years of stagnation. Last week the Commerce Department reported that the U.S. gross national product grew during the second quarter at an inflation-adjusted annual rate of 1.7%. Yet at the same time, the Government also sharply scaled back an earlier GNP estimate for the first quarter, reporting that the economy actually sank 5.1% on an annual basis during the January-to-March period instead of the initially estimated 3.7%. Moreover, the Bureau of Labor Statistics last week announced that consumer prices rose during June at a compound annual rate of 13.3% for the second month in a row.

J. P. Morgan (Source:BigCharts.com)

Same story, different crisis, different bank . . . same results.

Just when the market reaches its scariest moments, even amid fears of a systemic financial crisis, policy makers respond and the markets and economy bounce back.

As a very famous Wall Street investor told me in 1998, as Long-Term Capital Management was collapsing and everyone feared a stock-market crash and recession . . . "Bailouts Are Bullish!"

They were then and they are now.

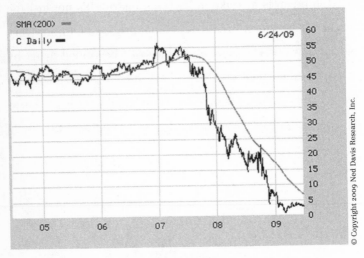

Citigroup (Source: BigCharts.com)

As in past crises, big banks such as Citi collapsed in value, almost to zero. And, as in the past, many were declaring the nation's biggest banks not only insolvent but poised to fail.

Failure of major financial institutions has grave economic consequences, as we witnessed with the collapse of Lehman Brothers and several other large firms. At the point of maximum pain and ultimate fear, in March 2009, the Feds simply could not allow another failure, or the system, both here and abroad, would have been torn apart.

Policy makers, as they have in prior crises, drew a line in

the sand and promised to halt the panic. Thus far they have been successful, despite the many skeptics who still believe that the financial system will fail.

Too much is at stake in such a scenario. It's not just the economic or the political environment that suffers, the very social fabric that holds us together can be ripped apart by an economic catastrophe. The Fed and the government are well aware of that, and have acted to avoid the direst consequences possible and will continue to do so until we are safely out of these woods.

Citigroup (Source: BigCharts.com)

So unless major banks literally fail, or are nationalized by the federal government, you can be princelike today and buy the banks at pauperlike prices.

As a consumer, you might fear that this looks more like a going-out-of-business sale than a bargain. But as I said, major banks simply will not be allowed to go bust. And if they do, our problems will be far greater, and we will be far poorer, compared to the losses we would suffer by taking a chance on Citigroup at historically low prices!

For Whom the Doorbell Tolls

Like banking stocks, the home builders have been crushed under the weight of a collapse in real estate. Describe it however you like—the roof caved in, the floor fell out, or the foundation was not solid—the housing industry has suffered its worst downturn in U.S. history.

Whether it is luxury builder Toll Brothers; the Ryland Group; the nation's largest home builder, K. Hovnanian; D.R. Horton; Pulte Homes; or Lennar; the stocks of all of these firms have approached levels reflecting the risk of imminent bankruptcy.

Some might still enter chapter 11, the casualties of historic overbuilding, lax lending standards, and buying excess land at inflated prices.

Others, such as Pulte and Centex, have chosen to merge. Still others are beginning to rebuild their businesses. They are offering attractive financing on new homes, in order to clear excess inventory. Some are buying back premium land at a discount, preparing for the next upturn in the housing cycle.

That could take a while, as you can see below. Housing starts, the number of homes where construction has begun, have not been this low in the postwar era. Housing starts have fallen 75 percent from their peak and are likely to rebound only slowly, according to most economists.

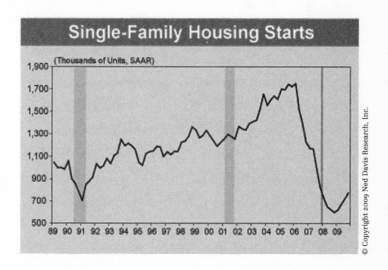

Despite that disturbing fact, and maybe not surprisingly, the National Association of Home Builders, the NAHB, calls the current housing environment "the opportunity of a lifetime" (www.nahb.org).

That may be true of housing stocks as well. In my portfolio, I own shares of Hovnanian, Toll Brothers, and Lennar.

Once again, I am betting on a rebound, not a further collapse. My logic is based on my study of market and economic

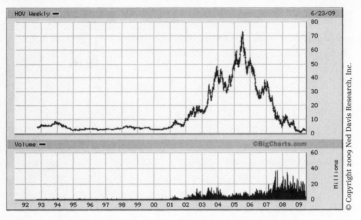

Hovnanian Enterprises (Source: BigCharts.com)

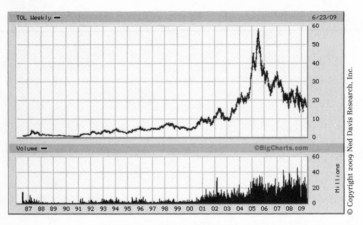

Toll Brothers (Source: BigCharts.com)

cycles. While I am taking a calculated risk here, given that any home builder can run into sufficient troubles to render its stocks worthless, they are not all going to zero, so I want to buy distressed housing stocks, as well as distressed real estate.

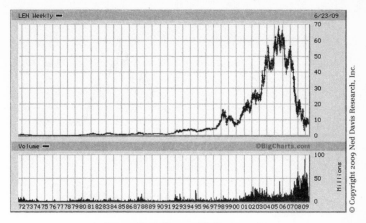

Lennar Corp. (Source: BigCharts.com)

Despite the extraordinary run-up in stock prices, which carried the S&P 500 to 40 percent above its March 9 lows, even beyond the banks and builders, the long-term picture for equities appears quite favorable to me.

The simplest way for you to take advantage of the downdraft in stocks is to buy proxies for the market, as I said earlier. Investors, however, may feel more comfortable with the do-it-yourself approach: building out a portfolio that is centered around the most beaten-down stocks, such as banks, home builders, large-cap techs, and other undervalued industries.

For so-called accredited investors, or qualified purchasers, who meet the requirements to invest in private-equity pools, hedge funds, and other sophisticated investment vehicles, I recommend going with the biggest names, those with the strongest track record in each category.

Because I worked in the hedge-fund industry for three years, investing with, and working for, some of the best names in the business, I remain conflicted as a consequence of those prior business relationships. I don't feel it appropriate to recommend specific names.

But the biggest and most well known investors—who take advantage of undervalued stocks, participate in "special situations," trade interest-rate swings, or go long and short the stock market—are among the most desirable professionals in the world of private equity and hedge funds.

Betting Right on REITS

Real estate investment trusts (REITS) have been the traditional way that an individual investor has taken advantage of property as an investment, as opposed to a place to live.

REITs are highly liquid securities that can be bought and sold on stock exchanges. They own a variety of different kinds of real estate.

There are, for example, REITs based on residential real estate—more specifically, multifamily housing, such as apartment buildings and other rental properties. In order to achieve certain tax benefits that go along with creating and marketing these REITs, the REITs manager must pay out 90 percent of the rents to shareholders.

The dividend payment on the REIT can offer individual

investors an attractive way to participate in the property markets, the same way individual investors can become part owners of multiple corporations by buying stock mutual funds, or bond investors can receive attractive interest payments on government or corporate bonds.

With REITs, the dividend payout is a key component of the return you receive. The average dividend on a REIT today is just about 8 percent. Assuming that there is no economic reason for a particular REIT to cut its dividend, an 8 percent yield means you could double your money with that investment in nine years, not counting any increase in the value of the REIT, if the property markets return to normal.

There are mortgage REITs that invest in property mortgages, from making direct loans to real estate owners, to buying mortgages in the open market or from banks, to buying and selling mortgage-backed securities, which are complex derivatives based on underlying mortgages or pools of mortgages.

There are also REITs that specialize in commercial real estate—specific real estate sectors, such as malls, health-care facilities, industrial land, or even hotels.

Since the bursting of the real estate bubble, REITs have been savaged in the marketplace—even the high-quality REITs, such as the trusts run by Sam Zell, legendary investor Ken Heebner, or real estate and media mogul Mort Zuckerman.

Let's go back to my old friend Sam Zell for a moment. His Equity Residential (EQR) is a great example of what I am talking about when it comes to REITs.

Equity Residential owns and manages the largest collection of apartment buildings and rental units in the country, making Sam the country's biggest landlord.

According to recent published reports, despite the troubles in real estate, EQR's properties are 94 percent occupied and rents have been quite stable. The dividend yield on EQR is above 8.5 percent, meaning that you'll receive an 8.5 percent return on your investment annually, assuming nothing goes wrong with the rental properties Sam owns.

The dividend yield, by the way, is the annual dividend divided by the REIT's market price. EQR, for instance, pays $1.92 in annual dividends, and its price, as I was writing this book, was $22.39. That results in a yield north of 8.5 percent.

The company has indicated it has no plans or reason to cut its payout—it has never done so since it came to market.

Some Wall Street analysts have been recommending EQR as a solid REIT investment, since its market price has plunged along with the rest of the real estate market, despite the stability of the underlying properties.

EQUITY RESIDENTIAL

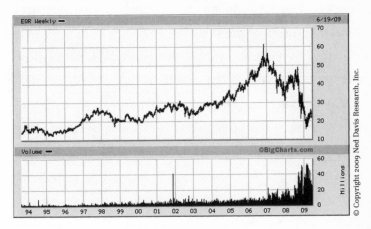

(Source: BigCharts.com)

Equity Residential's market price has fallen on hard times, even though its underlying fundamentals remain solid. As you can clearly see here, the REIT is trading at levels last seen in the late 1990s, well before the property market went bust.

This is not a recommendation for Sam's REIT. But the chart clearly illustrates that, like the underlying real estate market, REITs have been pounded.

Real estate values will not stay down forever, nor will the price of REITs. Buying a REIT with a generous, but not too generous, yield will not only offer potentially stable and attractive returns but also offer price appreciation, or a capital gain, if the world goes back to some version of normal. In the meantime, you are paid nearly 9 percent to wait.

I say that the yield, or more precisely the dividend yield, should not be too generous because, often, an extraordinary dividend yield could be a sign of trouble.

The dividend yield is, as explained earlier, the result of dividing the annual yield by the current market price of the REIT. When the dividend yield gets too high, it may indicate that the property manager is paying out an unsustainably large dividend. Think of it this way: the price of the REIT is falling because smart investors see trouble brewing in the REIT manager's underlying business. Without adjusting the payout downward, the dividend yield begins to rise. (If the price of the REIT is falling but the dividend stays the same, the dividend yield will rise automatically.)

But that rising yield could be signaling that the payout will need to be cut because the fundamentals of the underlying properties are deteriorating. That happened to some key mall REITS in 2009, as shopping centers went begging for customers and lessors.

General Growth Properties, which went bankrupt in 2009, sported a dividend yield of over 37 percent at its peak, but that was not an attractive yield—it was, instead, a sign of impending doom.

Like any investment, real estate investment trusts come with some attendant risks, not the least of which is how a recession, or real estate bust, can affect the underlying business.

But given the decimation of REIT values, many REITs are being recommended by financial market analysts as attractively priced, with solid yields and improving fundamentals.

The same can be said of closed-end mutual funds that invest in real estate, such as Ken Heebner's CGM Realty Fund.

Closed-end mutual funds trade on stock exchanges and also invest in real estate, seeking both attractive yields and capital appreciation.

CGM REALTY FUND

Ken Heebner is a multi-decade veteran of the investment wars. At the height of the 1990s mutual-fund mania, he was known as "the Mad Bomber" on Wall Street. He earned that reputation by dumping his entire holdings in a particular stock when he decided it was no longer an attractive investment.

The one-shot sale would drive the price of that stock down so hard that the folks on the floor of the New York Stock Exchange would immediately know it was the work of "the Mad Bomber."

Ken's CGM Realty Fund, which is a so-called no-load fund, has $894 million in assets, a yield of 4.7 percent, and like other like-minded REITs, has fallen well below its highest price levels.

Morningstar, a service that rates mutual funds, gives Ken's fund a five-star rating, its highest rank.

The fund has a minimum investment of $2,500 and has returned nearly 8 percent annually over the last five years. It had stellar returns in 2005, 2006, and 2007. But it lost nearly 47 percent of its value in 2008 and was down about 8 percent by mid-2009.

Unlike REITs, closed-end mutual funds, which can be bought and sold on the exchange but have a fixed amount of capital invested, will trade at a discount or a premium to their underlying net asset value, or NAV.

Typically, it is best to buy a closed-end fund that is trading at a discount to the value of the assets it owns and to sell it when it trades at a significant premium. The CGM Realty Fund is trading right around its NAV, which means, at least by that metric, it is neither too undervalued nor too overvalued. Trading, though, at less than half its all-time high, the fund will advance if and when real estate recovers.

I have watched Ken for many years now and have often found him to operate best when everyone else has given up on a particular asset class. Again, I don't want this to be construed as an explicit recommendation, just an example of where to find attractive real estate investments with well-established managers.

All the major mutual-fund companies, from Fidelity to Vanguard to T. Rowe Price, offer an array of mutual funds that focus on real estate investments. In reality, it is important to do your own research to find the type of real estate investment that best suits your needs and desires.

Morningstar, by the way, is the best service around when it comes to getting key information about all kinds of mutual-fund investments, from closed-end real estate funds to exchange-traded funds, ETFs, which continue to grow in popularity as investment vehicles.

In mid-2009, Morningstar mentioned the iShares NAREIT Mortgage Plus Capped Index (REM) as one of five "extreme" ETFs that are making big bets and "not for the faint of heart." According to Morningstar, REM is an exchange-traded fund that tracks an index that follows mortgage REITs.

Mortgage REITs or funds, as we noted, do not own property. They lend to property owners and acquire mortgages or mortgage-backed securities. These funds can use a lot of borrowed money, or leverage, to enhance their performance. Leverage is just Viagra for investors . . . you get the idea.

The risk with using leverage in investing—or any performance-enhancing substance, for that matter—is that it increases the volatility of the underlying investments, leading to wild swings in performance. If your investment goes up for more than four hours . . . you should immediately consult your broker . . . or something like that.

That said, REM, a leveraged ETF, is getting some attention from Morningstar as a real estate play that is not designed for widows and orphans, but for investors with a high tolerance for risk.

Data as of 06-19-2009 11:00 PM CT Price Graph		
Last Price $12.98	**Day Change** ▲ 0.19 (1.49%)	**Volume** 22,774
Open Price $12.91	**Day Range** 12.98–12.88	**52-Wk Range** 23.50–10.24
Bid/Ask 0.15/399.99	**Bid/Ask Spread** 199.85 %	**Prem/Discount** −1.31 % * * as of 06-19-2009

Morningstar

It is relatively new, unrated, and has promptly plunged from its offering price. Still, many investors and observers, myself included, are quite intrigued by the trading in mortgages and mortgage-backed securities, which have been crushed in value in the last two years but now are offering some attractive returns.

Now there are much more conventional ways to buy and sell real estate securities. Bloomberg keeps track of real estate ETFs on a daily basis, making it easy for you to follow.

Here's an example of a Bloomberg page that tracks real estate ETFs:

IYR: US iShares Dow Jones US Real Estate Index Fund
Objective: Sector Fund–Real Estate
06/19   Currency: USD

Price*	Change	% Change	52-Week High	52-Week Low	BETA vs.	Assets (Mil)
32.71	0.350	1.082	77.48 (09/19/08)	20.98 (03/06/09)	DJUSRE 0.97	1,402.75 (05/29/09)

Value for IYR: US Fund Profile

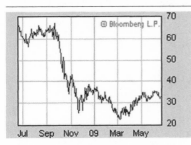

Chart the Performance of IYR:US

iShares Dow Jones U.S. Real Estate Index Fund is an exchange-traded fund incorporated in the USA. The Fund's objective seeks investment results that correspond to the performance of the Dow Jones U.S. Real Estate Index. The Fund will concentrate its investments in the real estate industry sector of the U.S. equity market to approximately the same extent the Index is so concentrated.

Fees

Front Load	Back Load	Redemption	Current Mgmt Fee	Expense Ratio	12b1 Fee
0.00	0.00	Fee 0.00	0.48	0.48	0.00

Current Returns

3-month	Year to Date	1-Year	3-Year	5-Year
27.09	−10.19	−47.03	−18.25	−3.82

5

A CRISIS IN CREDIT

BECAUSE OF THE MASSIVE CRISIS THAT GRIPPED THE CREDIT markets and caused the meltdown we have just been through, many types of bonds were hit extraordinarily hard, as investors all over the world dumped them, fearing a domino effect that would spread from the riskiest bonds to the highest-quality credits.

That's exactly what happened. The contagion from sub-prime mortgage bonds spread to other mortgages and mortgage derivatives, which in turn spread to so-called junk bonds (non-investment grade corporate bonds) to AAA corporate bonds to triple tax-free insured municipal bonds, and so on and so on.

The credit crisis froze the financial markets in place from late 2007 to early 2009, destroying values in every corner of the globe and forcing investors to sell bonds, whose ratings quality and values they could no longer calculate.

There has never been a seizing-up of markets like the one that took place in the recent past. Entire sectors of the markets literally shut down. Issuance of all kinds of bonds ceased, cutting off the supply of funds to banks, other financial institutions, and industrial companies alike, to towns and municipalities, and even to some sovereign governments.

Investment vehicles centered on mortgages collapsed in value. Banks and brokerages had to go to their respective governments to fund daily operations. Large industrial companies required federal assistance to borrow in the commercial paper markets to meet their short-term obligations. Cities, towns, and states saw interest rates skyrocket, limiting their ability to finance public-works projects or to budget shortfalls. Jefferson County, Alabama, went bankrupt, putting a punctuation mark on how serious, and contagious, the credit crisis was.

But that was the bad news. The good news is that the massive sell-off in bond investments made credit, particularly distressed credit, an extremely attractive investment arena.

It's true that in 2007 and 2008, many professional investors jumped in too soon and got annihilated trying to buy distressed credits at what turned out to be only "stressed" prices.

But today distressed is actually distressed, despite a recent improvement in credit conditions, and professional investors have begun building portfolios of distressed investments. Here, too, the government is providing assistance to investors willing to risk their money on "toxic," or troubled, assets.

Like the pros, individual investors now have many opportunities to take advantage of more-attractive yields in mortgage bonds, high-yield credits, municipal bonds, and "toxic" asset funds.

Several big bond investment companies, from Bill Gross's PIMCO to Black Rock to Legg Mason, are preparing funds like these. Some of the distressed-credit funds took a pounding in 2008 but are rebounding in 2009.

Along with them, the *Wall Street Journal* reported in April 2009 that Fidelity, Franklin Resources, and T. Rowe Price are exploring other federal programs that will allow them to create distressed-investment funds based on the government's Term Asset-Backed Securities Loan Facility, or TALF, which will invest in distressed consumer, small-business, and commercial-real-estate debt.

Some of the funds will be open to the general investing public, while others will have higher investment minimums and higher net worth, or income, requirements than normal mutual funds.

I believe that investing in distressed credit is the most attractive opportunity available today, especially if it is linked to government programs that provide support and incentives to the investment managers who are in effect helping the government clean up the toxic waste that resides on the books of our major banks.

While I don't expect the funds to be given preferential treatment, though that invariably happens, the investment firms helping out the government are going to get very favorable terms with which to buy these troubled assets, which will be a net benefit to the investors who put money to work in these funds.

Either through government assistance, or through the wreckage of the credit markets, opportunities abound for individuals again to profit, like pros, from market dislocations.

You may be worried that this credit stuff is way over your head. It's not. Many of you have been buying corporate or municipal bonds, for instance, for years. While it may take a little more homework to examine the credit risk associated with these investments, it's not that much harder to buy higher-yielding corporates and munis than it was before. But you are getting much richer compensation today than in years past for taking a slightly higher but calculated risk.

Against this backdrop, there is one kind of Treasury bond that should be the cornerstone of your credit portfolio, providing you some bedrock safety and a hedge against future inflation, should some of the government's stimulus programs work too well and create an inflationary problem down the road.

Many smart investors think that inflation is the most pressing long-term problem we will face, now that the government has flooded the economy with money to stave off a deflationary depression like that in the 1930s. While I only partially agree (I think deflation and recession are still the biggest near-term risks), I also own a substantial amount of Treasury Inflation-Protected Securities (TIPS) in my pension account, just in case the experts are right!

Take a TIP from Uncle Sam

Given that interest rates are at historic lows, I would be loath to recommend buying U.S. Treasury bonds at this juncture in the economic cycle. In the next several years, interest rates are more likely to go up than down, as the Fed eventually raises rates back to normal levels. Investors would lose money on their Treasury-bond holdings, since higher rates push bond prices down.

There is an inverse relationship between bond prices and bond yields. As interest rates rise, the prices of existing, lower-yielding Treasuries fall, as investors dump low-rate bonds to buy the new bonds with higher rates of interest.

As you know, on December 16, 2008, the Federal Reserve—in an emergency effort to stop the financial system from further melting down and taking the economy with it—cut short-term interest rates to between 0 and .25 percent.

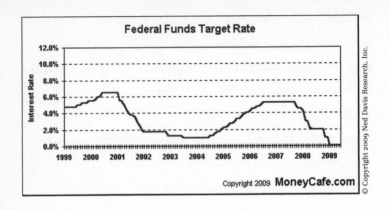

Official interest rates have never been lower, and the Fed has never experimented before with a zero-interest-rate policy.

If it works to revive the economy, the Fed will invariably, though not for some time to come, have to raise interest rates and begin to withdraw the trillions of dollars it has pushed into the economy to keep the credit crisis and recession from deepening.

That will make plain vanilla Treasury bonds less attractive. If the Fed fails to start raising rates and siphoning off the excess money in the system, it risks creating inflation—which makes Treasuries less attractive, as inflation eats away at the purchasing power of bond investments.

Here's why. Let's say you are earning 4 percent on a ten-year Treasury note. If inflation jumps to 5 percent, because the economy has strengthened and inflation is heating up, you are actually losing 1 percent in purchasing power each year.

Over the course of ten years, that makes your bond investment worth less and less and less. So not only does the yield fail to keep pace with inflation, but the value of the bond declines, leaving you with a large loss of principal!

The Fed is in an unenviable position in this regard since it has to choose between the lesser of two economic evils. If the Fed had not cut rates and poured trillions into the economy, the credit crisis would have most assuredly resulted in a deflationary depression.

But if the Fed allows the stimulants to stay in the system for too long, it will have to fight inflation sometime in the next several years, a challenge highlighted by former Fed chairman Alan Greenspan in the *Financial Times* on June 26, 2009.

But I see inflation as the greater future challenge. If political pressures prevent central banks from reining in their inflated balance sheets in a timely manner, statistical analysis suggests the emergence of inflation by 2012; earlier if markets anticipate a prolonged period of elevated money supply. Annual price inflation in the U.S. is significantly correlated (with a 3½-year lag) with annual changes in money supply per unit of capacity.

Inflation is a special concern over the next decade, given the pending avalanche of government debt about to be unloaded on world financial markets. The need to finance very large fiscal deficits during the coming years could lead to political pressure on central banks to print money to buy much of the newly issued debt.

Inflation by 2012! Despite my lack of attraction to regular Treasury bonds, I am, as I stated earlier, a holder of Treasury Inflation-Protected Securities, or TIPS.

TIPS, introduced by the Treasury during the second term of the Clinton administration, promise to pay bond investors a small nominal yield, plus a premium for rising inflation. It's kind of like the cost-of-living-adjustment (COLA) that Social Security recipients receive each year to adjust their monthly payments as inflation rises.

Inflation has actually fallen, year over year, from 2008 to 2009, for the first time since the 1950s. In the 1950s, deflation

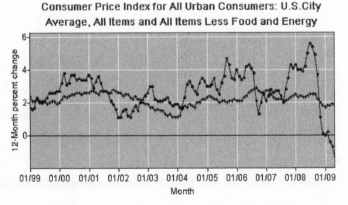

Consumer Price Index for All Urban Consumers: U.S.City Average, All Items and All Items Less Food and Energy

Source: Bureau of Labor Statistics, Consumer Price Indexes

was a favorable development that arose from strong economic growth and rising worker productivity. That kept prices in check, despite a postwar economic boom.

But falling inflation today is the result of a collapse in prices of assets, such as real estate, stocks, and bonds. That has caused a recession, not fueled economic growth.

As the Fed fights the forces of deflation, it risks, as Mr. Greenspan pointed out, overstimulating the economy and creating inflation, or possibly even hyperinflation.

That's where TIPS come in. These are Treasury bonds that protect you from the ravages of inflation. The interest-rate risk or inflation risk of owning regular Treasuries is taken away. And if interest rates can't go any lower than they already are, they will, by necessity, go up. That's why plain vanilla Treasuries are unattractive, but TIPS are a great buy.

You can buy TIPS from Treasury Direct by opening an account with the Federal Reserve Bank in your area of the country. There are twelve Federal Reserve districts in the United States, from New York to Dallas to San Francisco.

By buying directly from the Treasury, through the Fed, you save on brokerage commissions. Why is that important? It's very important because bond brokers bury their fees in the price of the bond. In other words, instead of paying a price of 100 for a newly issued bond, you may pay 104, which your broker will tell you is normal. It's not. He's packing four points of commission into your costs, up front, cutting into your returns.

So if you are going to buy TIPS—and I recommend a blend of five-, ten-, and twenty-year maturities—buy from Treasury Direct. The minimums are usually between $5,000 and $10,000, but the cost savings can be enormous!

That is true of all Treasury bonds, by the way. Going direct is the best, most cost-effective option.

Municipal Bonds

There was no investment arena that was more surprisingly weakened by the credit crisis than municipal bonds. Long one of the simplest, safest, and most reliable investments available, insured tax-free municipal bonds were unexpectedly, and severely, punished by the goings-on in the most arcane corners of the credit markets.

However, municipal bonds, according to many experts, are now among the most attractive investments available to individual investors!

It came as a shock to everyone that the financing of schools, waste-treatment facilities, and state and local governments would be so adversely affected by a crisis that had its roots in real estate lending, mortgage-related derivatives, and sub-prime paper.

But that is exactly what happened, for reasons that only a very few were familiar with. And those areas were far more inextricably linked than anyone had ever realized.

According to WM Financial Strategies, a municipal bond advisory firm in St. Louis, triple-A municipal bond insurance began with Ambac in 1971. By 2007, Ambac, MBIA, and other insurance firms had covered about $1.25 trillion worth of municipal bonds, while other firms, such as Radian Group, insured lesser-quality municipal bonds.

But in recent years that mundane business of insuring municipal bonds morphed into an even larger business, through some regulatory loopholes, which allowed those simple shops to begin insuring complex mortgage derivatives, such as CDOs and other complicated structures. Neither they, nor too many others, fully understood the calamities that would ultimately befall them when the bottom dropped out of the housing market.

The simple fact is this: The firms that had insured municipal bonds against the loss of both principal and interest had, unbeknownst to the investing public, entered a new business in the last several years, insuring the highly risky derivatives that we discussed before—CDOs and other pools of mortgage-related investment securities.

When that market crashed, the size of the liabilities was so big that bond insurers—such as MBIA, Ambac, and others—simply did not have the capital to cover those losses and still have adequate reserves to cover potential losses in municipal bonds.

What was thought to be insured against losses was effectively uninsured after the crash. The simple, safe "widows and orphans" bonds that allowed state and local governments to build highways, sewage-treatment facilities, bridges, tunnels, and hospitals were suddenly fraught with risk. Investors dumped them en masse, causing their prices to plummet and their yields to soar.

Adding insult to injury were so-called auction-rate securities, ARS, which were pools of municipal bonds that provided weekly liquidity to investors who wished to park their money in a "cash equivalent" that had higher yields than bank CDs or money-market mutual funds.

Typically, the big investment banks that underwrote the securities would buy any bonds that were not snapped up by the public, effectively supporting the market for these securities. But after the credit crash, the banks stopped supporting the ARS market. The market froze, and customers wishing to redeem their funds had their accounts frozen for many months.

These "cash equivalents" turned out not to be so readily available, further shrinking the pool of funds that were lent to municipalities and exacerbating the run on munis.

To complicate matters even further, this recession has deprived state and local governments of both income and property tax receipts, creating big budget deficits for as many as forty-eight of the fifty states, totaling about $166 billion, according to a June 29, 2009, report from the Center on Budget and Policy Priorities. The center projects that shortfall to grow to $180 billion in fiscal 2010!

California's fiscal crisis was the most serious, with a yawning budget gap of $24 billion, followed by New York at nearly $18 billion and New Jersey at nearly $9 billion.

As a consequence, ratings agencies have downgraded municipal bonds and raised their cost of borrowing.

But that's the bad news. The good news is that muni bonds are providing yields that are quite generous, tax free (triple tax free if you buy them from the state you live in), and relatively safe, if you buy general obligation bonds as opposed to specific project bonds.

No state has gone bankrupt in the history of the Union. And while the likes of California, and possibly a handful of other cash-strapped states, have issued or may issue IOUs rather than interest payments to bondholders, while they sort out their budget crises, smart investors like Warren Buffett have been increasing their exposure to muni bonds throughout 2009.

After issuing IOUs to cover expenses in mid-2009, California's credit rating was cut to near-junk status by Fitch Investors Services, a bond-rating agency.

Cumberland Advisors, a billion-dollar money-management firm that, among other things, specializes in municipal-bond investments, says California's bonds are looking quite attractive and that any long-term paper from the Golden State with a yield of 6.5 percent is pure gold! The same, they say, is true for ten-year California bonds, with yields above 5 percent.

John Mousseau, of Cumberland, noted in a July 6, 2009, report that in 1992, at the end of a difficult housing-led recession in California, and a similar budget crisis, California governor Pete Wilson also issued IOUs to cover expenses while the nutty California legislature tried to overcome a similar budget impasse.

The impasse was resolved, the recession passed, and the bonds issued at that time were also bargains.

Mousseau reminded his readers of the *Grapes of Wrath* version of the Depression, in which half of Oklahoma migrated to California, as the Dust Bowl was disproportionately affected. He quoted Will Rogers, who remarked at the time, " 'During the Depression half the population of Oklahoma moved to California, and the intelligence level in both states went up.' " Mousseau added, "What Rogers forgot to note is that all the migrants are now in the legislature."

Some municipal bonds, in other cash-strapped states, are now also yielding in excess of 6 percent or 7 percent, tax-free! If you make $50,000 a year, that is equal to a 7.25 percent to 8 percent taxable yield. If you are in the top tax bracket, the taxable equivalent yield is over 10 percent!

Most discount brokers and electronic trading platforms, such as TD Ameritrade or E*Trade (which I own in my portfolio), provide research tools and screens that can be used to select the kinds of bonds you want.

They do that with stocks, mutual funds, and ETFs as well.

The one suggestion I would offer, as you explore municipal bonds, is to take note of the credit risk of the issuer. State general obligation bonds (GOs) are among the safest types of municipal bonds, as I suggested earlier. States do not go bankrupt, and general obligation bonds are among the most senior and secure credits issued by states. In a state like California, for instance, they must pay their general obligation bonds just after they cover the costs of funding their schools, which puts the GOs second in the creditor stack. Even in the current distressed environment, it would be highly unlikely for even a debt-ridden state like California to default on its GOs. (On July 23, 2009, Governor Arnold Schwarzenegger and state lawmakers solved the $26 billion budget impasse, making California's general obligation bonds that much more attractive.)

Before buying the bonds of any state that might be downgraded by a ratings agency, I would wait until *after* the downgrade and then pick up the munis at a deep discount. That's yet another way to take advantage of the distress currently afflicting the credit markets.

Picking the right bond takes a little homework. Your choice is affected by your tax bracket, the state in which you live, and a variety of other factors. I am using these pages as examples of the kinds of municipal bonds available. They are not being recommended for purchase.

Your financial planner can help you pick the bond or bonds that best suit you and find a broker who will not overcharge you for the bond by, again, burying a fat commission in the price.

Municipal bonds are getting more and more attractive as tax rates move up and yields rise to offset the declining fortunes of many state and local issuers.

While I am concerned that more and more states are suffering financially, I believe they will take the steps, and some of them will be extraordinary, to balance their books and right their teetering ships.

Here's a sampling, for illustrative purposes only, of what a muni-bond screen looks like on TD Ameritrade:

CUSIP	Qty / Min	Issue
720175MM7 SC	15 15	PIEDMONT MUN PWR AGY S C ELEC ELEC REV REF BD ELEC & PUB PWR REV ALL BONDS Ser 1993, OID: 98.838, Non Callable, Escrowed To Maturity
720175MM7 SC	15 15	PIEDMONT MUN PWR AGY S C ELEC ELEC REV REF BD ELEC & PUB PWR REV ALL BONDS Ser 1993, OID: 98.838, Non Callable, Escrowed To Maturity
89602NHF4 NY	5 5	TRIBOROUGH BRDG & TUNL AUTH N GEN PURP REV BD BRIDGES REV ALL BONDS Ser 2001 A, OID: 98.614, Pre-refunded 01-01-2012 @ 100.000, MANDATORY SINKING FUND
13062N5M5 CA	10 10	CALIFORNIA ST G.O. BDS GEN PURP/PUB IMPT ULT G.O. ALL BONDS Ser 2002, OID: 95.952, Pre-refunded 02-01-2012 @ 100.000, MANDATORY SINKING FUND
7178807D4 PA	700 50	PHILADELPHIA PA SCH DIST G.O. BDS PRIM/SECNDRY ED ULT G.O. ALL BONDS Ser 2002A, Pre-refunded 02-01-2012 @ 100.000, MANDATORY SINKING FUND
880541AP2 TN	1000 50	TENNESSEE ST G.O. BDS GEN PURP/PUB IMPT ULT G.O. ALL BONDS Ser 2002 A, Pre-refunded 02-01-2012 @ 100.000

That's what it looks like to buy bonds directly, via an electronic trading platform. You still need to do research on muni bonds on your own.

Some are triple-A rated, while others are riskier credits. Some have the money owed to investors put in an escrow account to ensure payment, while others are insured against loss of your principal or interest.

You can find screens like these for stocks, mutual funds, and ETFs as well.

Coupon Org. Maturity	Maturity / Ratings	YTM* YTW	Price
5.500 01-01-2012	01-01-2012 Baa1/A	1.659 Mat	109.316
5.500 01-01-2012	01-01-2012 Baa1/A	1.659 Mat	109.316
5.000 01-01-2032	01-01-2012 Aa2/AAA	0.680 Pre Ref	110.633
5.000 02-01-2032	02-01-2012 A2/AAA	1.236 Pre Ref	109.490
5.500 02-01-2031	02-01-2012 Aa3/AAA	0.613 Pre Ref	112.439
5.000 02-01-2016	02-01-2012 Aa1/AA+	0.464 Pre Ref	111.571

CUSIP	Qty / Min	Issue
074358DA7 SC	25 5	BEAUFORT-JASPER S C WTR & SWR IMPT & REV BDS WTR & SWR REV ALL BONDS Proj SECOND LIEN Ser 2001, OID: 97.658, Pre-refunded 03-01-2012 @ 100.000, MANDATORY SINKING FUND
13062T3G7 CA	5 5	CALIFORNIA ST G.O. BDS GEN PURP/PUB IMPT ULT G.O. ALL BONDS Ser 2002, OID: 96.947, Pre-refunded 04-01-2012 @ 100.000, MANDATORY SINKING FUND
684545RR9 FL	5 5	ORANGE CNTY FLA TOURIST DEV TA TOURIST DEV TA REDEV/LD CLEARANCE REV ALL BONDS Ser 2002, OID: 96.586, Pre-refunded 04-01-2012 @ 100.000, MANDATORY SINKING FUND
684545RP3 FL	10 10	ORANGE CNTY FLA TOURIST DEV TA TOURIST DEV TA REDEV/LD CLEARANCE REV ALL BONDS Ser 2002, OID: 97.346, Pre-refunded 04-01-2012 @ 100.000
684545RR9 FL	2250 50	ORANGE CNTY FLA TOURIST DEV TA TOURIST DEV TA REDEV/LD CLEARANCE REV ALL BONDS Ser 2002, OID: 96.586, Pre-refunded 04-01-2012 @ 100.000, MANDATORY SINKING FUND
684545RQ1 FL	5000 50	ORANGE CNTY FLA TOURIST DEV TA TOURIST DEV TA REDEV/LD CLEARANCE REV ALL BONDS Ser 2002, OID: 98.889, Pre-refunded 04-01-2012 @ 100.000
684545RH1 FL	10 5	ORANGE CNTY FLA TOURIST DEV TA TOURIST DEV TA REDEV/LD CLEARANCE REV ALL BONDS Ser 2002, OID: 97.642, Pre-refunded 04-01-2012 @ 100.000
684545RG3 FL	25 5	ORANGE CNTY FLA TOURIST DEV TA TOURIST DEV TA REDEV/LD CLEARANCE REV ALL BONDS Ser 2002, OID: 98.170, Pre-refunded 04-01-2012 @ 100.000
684545RK4 FL	5 5	ORANGE CNTY FLA TOURIST DEV TA TOURIST DEV TA REDEV/LD CLEARANCE REV ALL BONDS Ser 2002, OID: 98.441, Pre-refunded 04-01-2012 @ 100.000
846851DA8 SC	10 5	SPARTANBURG CNTY S C HEALTH SV REF REV BDS HOSPITALS REV ALL BONDS Ser 2002, OID: 98.357, Pre-refunded 04-15-2012 @ 100.000, MANDATORY SINKING FUND, Extraordinary Redemption Provisions
088563SJ1 TX	1425 50	BEXAR TEX MET WTR DIST WTRWKS REV BDS WATER REV ALL BONDS Ser 2002, Pre-refunded 05-01-2012 @ 100.000
13066YKQ1 CA	500 50	CALIFORNIA ST DEPT WTR RES PWR WTR RES PWR SU ELEC & PUB PWR REV ALL BONDS Ser 2002 A, OID: 99.207, Pre-refunded 05-01-2012 @ 101.000

Coupon Org. Maturity	Maturity / Ratings	YTM* YTW	Price
5.000 03-01-2026	03-01-2012 Aa2/AAA	0.889 Pre Ref	110.753
5.000 04-01-2027	04-01-2012 A2/AAA	1.110 Pre Ref	110.452
5.125 10-01-2030	04-01-2012 A2/BBB	1.300 Pre Ref	110.246
5.125 10-01-2026	04-01-2012 A2/BBB	1.460 Pre Ref	109.792
5.125 10-01-2030	04-01-2012 A2/BBB	0.752 Pre Ref	111.821
5.250 10-01-2027	04-01-2012 A2/BBB	0.751 Pre Ref	112.160
5.000 10-01-2020	04-01-2012 A2/BBB	1.066 Pre Ref	110.578
5.000 10-01-2019	04-01-2012 A2/BBB	1.208 Pre Ref	110.174
5.125 10-01-2022	04-01-2012 A2/BBB	1.042 Pre Ref	110.985
5.250 04-15-2027	04-15-2012 Aa3/AAA	1.169 Pre Ref	111.109
5.375 05-01-2019	05-01-2012 Aa3/AAA	0.769 Pre Ref	112.822
5.125 05-01-2018	05-01-2012 Aa3/A+	0.370 Pre Ref	114.313

CUSIP	Qty / Min	Issue
251129ZQ8 MI	350 5	DETROIT MICH CITY SCH DIST G.O. SCHOOL BDS PRIM/SECNDRY ED ULT G.O. ALL BONDS Ser 2001A, Pre-refunded 05-01-2012 @ 100.000
709141WF8 PA	400 50	PENNSYLVANIA ST G.O. BDS GEN PURP/PUB IMPT ULT G.O. ALL BONDS Ser 2ND OF 2002, Pre-refunded 05-01-2012 @ 100.000
709141WH4 PA	2850 50	PENNSYLVANIA ST G.O. BDS GEN PURP/PUB IMPT ULT G.O. ALL BONDS Ser 2ND OF 2002, Pre-refunded 05-01-2012 @ 100.000
709141WG6 PA	150 50	PENNSYLVANIA ST G.O. BDS GEN PURP/PUB IMPT ULT G.O. ALL BONDS Ser 2ND OF 2002, Pre-refunded 05-01-2012 @ 100.000
759858AM5 NV	125 50	RENO NEV SALES & ROOM TAX REV SALES & TAX REV MASS/RAPID TRAN REV ALL BONDS Proj RETRAC-RENO RAIL ACCESS CORRID Ser 2002, OID: 96.455, Pre-refunded 06-01-2012 @ 100.000, MANDATORY SINKING FUND
759858AN3 NV	5 5	RENO NEV SALES & ROOM TAX REV SALES & TAX REV MASS/RAPID TRAN REV ALL BONDS Proj RETRAC-RENO RAIL ACCESS CORRID Ser 2002, OID: 97.725, Pre-refunded 06-01-2012 @ 100.000, MANDATORY SINKING FUND
646135SG9 NJ	4000 50	NEW JERSEY ST TRANSN TR FD AUT TRANSN SYS REV OTHER TRANSN REV ALL BONDS Proj TRANSN SYS Ser 2000 A, Non Callable, Escrowed To Maturity

I should also point out that there are new federal bonds, subsidized by Washington, which are being used by the government to build roads, bridges, and schools.

These Build America Bonds (see Bloomberg News, 6/25/2009) are taxable, compete with tax-free munis by paying higher rates than corporate bonds do, and may very well be used to reduce the size of the tax-free market. The "Obama Bonds," as they are being referred to, may also be used to shrink the muni market so that wealthy Americans cannot

Coupon Org. Maturity	Maturity / Ratings	YTM* YTW	Price
5.500 05-01-2015	05-01-2012 Aa3/AAA	0.975 Pre Ref	112.554
5.500 05-01-2017	05-01-2012 Aa2/AAA	1.012 Pre Ref	112.441
5.500 05-01-2019	05-01-2012 Aa2/AAA	0.618 Pre Ref	113.622
5.500 05-01-2018	05-01-2012 Aa2/AAA	0.618 Pre Ref	113.622
5.125 06-01-2037	06-01-2012 Baa3/BBB	1.176 Pre Ref	111.235
5.250 06-01-2041	06-01-2012 Baa3/BBB	1.535 Pre Ref	110.506
6.000 06-15-2012	06-15-2012 Aa3/AAA	0.588 Mat	115.760

reduce their tax bills—a maneuver reportedly disliked by the president.

The size of the "Obama Bond" market, at $14.4 billion, pales in comparison to the $2.7 trillion tax-free muni market. But as ever, we must keep a close eye on Washington to see how policy affects the opportunities set in front of us.

Again, I would consult with a financial planner to make sure that any tax-free muni bond you buy won't be affected, or made less attractive, by these new bonds.

Making the Grade

Investment-grade corporate bonds also have become quite an interesting investment since the credit crisis reached its crescendo at the end of 2008 and beginning of 2009. The spread between high-quality (as opposed to high-yield) corporate bonds widened to more than six percentage points over Treasury bonds of similar maturities. That was the widest gap ever recorded between Treasury yields and corporate-bond yields, despite the fact that many of these bonds were rated AAA!

The mauling of high-quality debt allowed corporate bonds to return more than 9 percent in the first half of 2009, as seasoned bond managers took advantage of the attractive yields to scoop up these issues at discounted prices.

Atop the safety spectrum among corporate bonds are the credits of big banks and financial companies that, during the height of the economic crisis, had their bonds backed by the Federal Deposit Insurance Corporation (FDIC). These bonds are guaranteed for three years from the date of issue. The FDIC was going to guarantee bank bonds for up to ten years, but recently scrapped that plan as credit markets improved and corporations were able, by mid-2009, to raise funds in the capital markets without government assistance.

Among the corporate bonds available, these are the safest. Their yields are among the lowest, but they are still a very interesting bond bet, with the full faith and credit of the U.S. government behind them.

Like stocks, corporate bonds were anticipating Armageddon, and like stocks, rebounded when the end of the world didn't come. But many corporate bonds are still trading at discounts and could make quite attractive investments.

These higher-quality, investment-grade bonds are generally safer than high-yield bonds, as they are issued by companies likely to survive the recession and thrive in the next upturn.

On the following pages is a sampling of some bonds rated "BBB" and above, from brand-name companies that sport relatively generous yields with relatively little risk. (Remember the brand-name discount Web site I showed you earlier? This sampling, from TD Ameritrade, shows some well-known corporate bonds with solid yields.)

Make sure you consult with a financial advisor to verify that the bonds are priced fairly and do not have a hefty brokerage commission embedded in the purchase price!

Note: In some cases, Moody's reports may show a different name than the offering—this may be due to a corporate name change.

CUSIP	Qty / Min	Issue
035229CU5 Industrial	10 5	ANHEUSER BUSCH COS INC Non Callable, Make Whole Calls, NYBE, BUD
035229CU5 Industrial	15 15	ANHEUSER BUSCH COS INC Non Callable, Make Whole Calls, NYBE, BUD
035229CU5 Industrial	150 10	ANHEUSER BUSCH COS INC Non Callable, Make Whole Calls, NYBE, BUD
136375BS0 Transportation	367 10	CANADIAN NATL RY CO Non Callable, Make Whole Calls, NYBE, CNI
22541LAM5 Financial	100 5	CREDIT SUISSE USA INC Non Callable, Spec Redemp, NYBE, CS
22541LAM5 Financial	39 10	CREDIT SUISSE USA INC Non Callable, Spec Redemp, NYBE, CS
25179MAG8 Industrial	963 5	DEVON ENERGY CORP NEW Non Callable, Make Whole Calls, NYBE
25179MAG8 Industrial	200 5	DEVON ENERGY CORP NEW Non Callable, Make Whole Calls, NYBE
25179MAG8 Industrial	200 20	DEVON ENERGY CORP NEW Non Callable, Make Whole Calls, NYBE
25243YAN9 Industrial	900 5	DIAGEO CAP PLC Non Callable, Make Whole Calls, Spec Redemp, NYBE
25243YAN9 Industrial	100 5	DIAGEO CAP PLC Non Callable, Make Whole Calls, Spec Redemp, NYBE
25243YAN9 Industrial	50 5	DIAGEO CAP PLC Non Callable, Make Whole Calls, Spec Redemp, NYBE
25243YAN9 Industrial	100 10	DIAGEO CAP PLC Non Callable, Make Whole Calls, Spec Redemp, NYBE
263534BV0 Industrial	20 5	DU PONT E I DE NEMOURS & CO Non Callable, Make Whole Calls, Spec Redemp, NYBE
263534BV0 Industrial	1036 10	DU PONT E I DE NEMOURS & CO Non Callable, Make Whole Calls, Spec Redemp, NYBE
263534BV0 Industrial	187 20	DU PONT E I DE NEMOURS & CO Non Callable, Make Whole Calls, Spec Redemp, NYBE

Coupon	Maturity / Ratings	YTM YTW	Price	Action
4.950	01-15-2014 Baa2/BBB+ Moody's Report	4.180 Mat	103.142	Buy
4.950	01-15-2014 Baa2/BBB+ Moody's Report	4.267 Mat	102.783	Buy
4.950	01-15-2014 Baa2/BBB+ Moody's Report	4.276 Mat	102.745	Buy
4.950	01-15-2014 A3/A- Moody's Report	3.418 Mat	106.369	Buy
5.125	01-15-2014 Aa1/A+ Moody's Report	3.836 Mat	105.306	Buy
5.125	01-15-2014 Aa1/A+ Moody's Report	4.166 Mat	103.914	Buy
5.625	01-15-2014 Baa1/BBB+ Moody's Report	3.931 Mat	106.956	Buy
5.625	01-15-2014 Baa1/BBB+ Moody's Report	3.702 Mat	107.940	Buy
5.625	01-15-2014 Baa1/BBB+ Moody's Report	3.903 Mat	107.074	Buy
7.375	01-15-2014 A3/A- Moody's Report	3.277 Mat	117.092	Buy
7.375	01-15-2014 A3/A- Moody's Report	3.419 Mat	116.444	Buy
7.375	01-15-2014 A3/A- Moody's Report	3.377 Mat	116.636	Buy
7.375	01-15-2014 A3/A- Moody's Report	3.510 Mat	116.030	Buy
5.875	01-15-2014 A2/A Moody's Report	3.502 Mat	109.842	Buy
5.875	01-15-2014 A2/A Moody's Report	3.565 Mat	109.569	Buy
5.875	01-15-2014 A2/A Moody's Report	3.263 Mat	110.897	Buy

CUSIP	Qty / Min	Issue
263534BV0 Industrial	464 5	DU PONT E I DE NEMOURS & CO Non Callable, Make Whole Calls, Spec Redemp, NYBE
263534BV0 Industrial	646 5	DU PONT E I DE NEMOURS & CO Non Callable, Make Whole Calls, Spec Redemp, NYBE
263534BV0 Industrial	100 5	DU PONT E I DE NEMOURS & CO Non Callable, Make Whole Calls, Spec Redemp, NYBE
38143UAB7 Financial	595 5	GOLDMAN SACHS GROUP INC Non Callable, Spec Redemp, NYBE, GS
38143UAB7 Financial	180 5	GOLDMAN SACHS GROUP INC Non Callable, Spec Redemp, NYBE, GS
38143UAB7 Financial	500 5	GOLDMAN SACHS GROUP INC Non Callable, Spec Redemp, NYBE, GS
38143UAB7 Financial	230 10	GOLDMAN SACHS GROUP INC Non Callable, Spec Redemp, NYBE, GS
38143UAB7 Financial	375 15	GOLDMAN SACHS GROUP INC Non Callable, Spec Redemp, NYBE, GS
38143UAB7 Financial	292 10	GOLDMAN SACHS GROUP INC Non Callable, Spec Redemp, NYBE, GS

From the likes of Goldman Sachs, the "king of Wall Street," to Anheuser-Busch, maker of the "king of beers," these are high-quality companies whose bonds have reasonably attractive and safe yields. They are good choices for those who are risk averse and would prefer to benefit from the distressed bond market, without the stress of traveling too far out on the risk curve.

On other sites, like those of money-management powerhouses Fidelity, Vanguard, and others, you can find discounted

Coupon	Maturity / Ratings	YTM YTW	Price	Action
5.875	01-15-2014 A2/A Moody's Report	3.401 Mat	110.286	Buy
5.875	01-15-2014 A2/A Moody's Report	3.431 Mat	110.157	Buy
5.875	01-15-2014 A2/A Moody's Report	3.194 Mat	111.203	Buy
5.150	01-15-2014 A1/A Moody's Report	4.481 Mat	102.708	Buy
5.150	01-15-2014 A1/A Moody's Report	4.544 Mat	102.452	Buy
5.150	01-15-2014 A1/A Moody's Report	4.355 Mat	103.231	Buy
5.150	01-15-2014 A1/A Moody's Report	4.485 Mat	102.692	Buy
5.150	01-15-2014 A1/A Moody's Report	4.464 Mat	102.781	Buy
5.150	01-15-2014 A1/A Moody's Report	4.464 Mat	102.778	Buy

bonds from Household Finance, Bank of America, and GE Capital that sport yields of anywhere from 5.6 percent all the way to 7.25 percent, with maturities as short as six years to maturities as long as fourteen years.

It is likely that, while challenged today, all of these companies will survive and pay back the bonds, as required and desired.

One thing I would point out, and this is true of all asset classes except physical real estate, is that from March 2009 through June 2009, many of these investments had extra-ordinary run-ups in price. That's something I mentioned in the risk/reward section of this book.

I spoke with Gregory Nassour, who runs the $36 billion investment-grade bond business for Vanguard, one of the nation's top mutual-fund managers. While he still thinks corporate credit is a good buy, he cautions that a lot of the "easy money" was made during the March–June 2009 period.

The so-called recovery trade, which allowed stocks, bonds, and commodities to step back from the brink of utter collapse, produced a very powerful rally as "Armageddon" was priced out of the markets.

Still, he thinks a diversified basket of investment-grade and some non-investment-grade bonds will provide investors with very ample returns over the next two years, at the least.

He predicts that many institutions—such as insurance companies, which must invest their cash to generate large enough returns to cover future liabilities—will be forced to "stretch for yield." That means that since Treasury bills, notes, and bonds yield so little, investors must move out on the "risk curve" and buy corporate bonds that have higher yields.

As a consequence, Nassour believes, the second round of buying in corporate bonds will be demand driven, which in turn will push prices higher, allowing for further capital appreciation along with some fat interest-rate payments. Nassour also expects corporations to continue issuing new debt as the credit markets continue their improvement. According to Bloomberg, at least 262 big U.S. companies issued $301 billion of investment-grade debt, taking advantage of extremely low interest rates, even if they didn't need the money immediately.

Even high-quality bonds can produce sizable returns, particularly if you find a low-cost, well-run mutual fund that specializes in buying, trading, and/or holding investment-grade corporate debt.

Professional fund managers, such as Nassour, who know how to take advantage of price discrepancies in the new-issue market, can also improve your returns if you let them handle that chore via a mutual-fund investment. Frequently, corporate-bond fund managers will mix high-quality debt with lesser-quality issues and a little junk paper to increase the returns of the fund.

That type of asset-allocation is best left to the pros, as they do all the homework for you.

Put Some Junk in Your Trunk!

OK, I admit that's a little more hip than I am entitled to be. But investors should be prepared to buy high-yield bonds to capture what are some of the most attractive junk-bond yields in history.

This game can be a great deal trickier than buying

high-quality corporate debt of companies with solid earnings prospects, clean balance sheets, and few business problems. High-yield debt offers high yields because the companies are facing some serious difficulties, and investors demand a premium yield as protection from potential defaults or bankruptcy.

However, in this credit crisis and recession, junk-bond yields have soared to their highest levels ever relative to the safest comparable Treasury bonds (that is, Treasury bonds with the same maturities), making this one of the best opportunities in the high-yield sector we've ever seen. The record high yields in junk bonds are predicting default rates well above the likely number of bankruptcies that will actually take place. That means that junk bonds are mispriced. They are too cheap relative to the prospects for further deterioration. In that sense, they are a "buy," despite the rally they have enjoyed since March of 2009.

Junk bonds were made famous in the 1980s by the "Junk Bond King," Michael Milken, who initially used non-investment-grade debt to finance a host of start-up industries, from cable TV to cellular phones to high-tech firms. Eventually, however, junk bonds were used to finance hostile takeovers of companies and to finance leveraged buyouts, or LBOs.

The over-leveraging of corporate America in the late 1980s, from RJR Nabisco to Northwest Airlines, led to a credit crisis not unlike the one we're experiencing today. Heavily indebted companies defaulted on that debt, or went bankrupt, in the recession of the early 1990s, saddling banks with mountains of bad buyout debt and exacerbating the recession.

What was interesting, however, was that many of Milken's former compatriots started companies that invested in the even higher-yielding debt that was used to finance those deals after the LBO craze blew up. They made a fortune buying the debt of those companies at pennies on the dollar, restructured the companies, and got even wealthier than they were when they were leveraging up the companies in the first place.

All this happened while Milken was serving an eighteen-month sentence in jail for a variety of market abuses and his former firm, Drexel Burnham Lambert, went belly up itself.

Today, yields on junk bonds are even higher, though there are many risks associated with buying high-yield debt.

As a consequence of this being the worst recession since the 1930s, the annualized default rate on junk debt is at an all-time high, at about 20 percent.

As a result, junk-bond yields, at the height of the credit crisis, traded about 20 percentage points over comparable Treasuries. That gap has narrowed to about 11 percentage points, as the junk-bond market rallied along with stocks and other so-called risk assets. This is shown in the chart on the following page, from the June 29, 2009, edition of the *Wall Street Journal*.

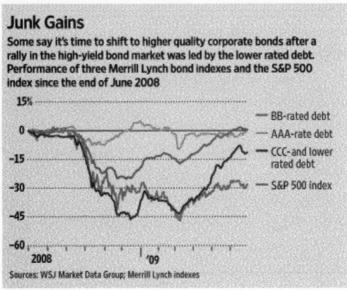

Junk Gains

Some say it's time to shift to higher quality corporate bonds after a rally in the high-yield bond market was led by the lower rated debt. Performance of three Merrill Lynch bond indexes and the S&P 500 index since the end of June 2008

- BB-rated debt
- AAA-rate debt
- CCC- and lower rated debt
- S&P 500 index

Sources: WSJ Market Data Group; Merrill Lynch indexes

From *The Wall Street Journal*. Reprinted by permission of "How to Make a Fortune from the Biggest Bailout in U.S. History," © Copyright 2009 Dow Jones & Company, Inc. All Rights Reserved Worldwide. License number 2259530041618.

The *Journal* noted that the rally may prove to be a trap, since default rates continue to rise, and that the lower yields resulting from the 2009 rally may offer less protection against that risk.

However, professional money managers should be used to taking that risk on your behalf. Rather than suggest that you buy Treasury Bonds on your own, as I recommended earlier, I would strongly urge you to use actively managed mutual funds for your high-yield investments.

According to KDP Investment Advisors, which does intensive research on high-yield debt, junk bonds remain attractive investments. KDP says the average rate paid on a basket of high-yield bonds that mature in 2014 is about 7.75 percent. That is a hefty return, although not without risk. These are B-rated bonds, so they are not pure junk; however, they are not the highest quality, either.

Let's get familiar with how Morningstar can help you find the right high-yield fund, one that takes into account your risk tolerance and your return objectives in this category of fund.

Morningstar identifies newly minted top-rated, high-yield bond funds. It also analyzes other funds that are either conservative junk funds (yes, I know it's an oxymoron) or even riskier offerings, and rates the following as five-star funds: Vanguard High-Yield Corporate (VWEHX); T.Rowe Price High-Yield (PRHYX); Buffalo High-Yield (BUFHX); Fidelity Advisor High-Income Advantage (FAHYX); and PIMCO High-Yield (PHDAX). And Morningstar tracks the top performers in each bond-fund universe. See pages 130–31 for the top eleven in mid-2009.

If, however, you'd like to do it yourself, electronic brokers and discount brokers offer screens that allow you to find high-yield funds, among other investments, and trade directly from their sites.

TD Ameritrade, one of the platforms I use, has twenty-seven pages of high-yield funds to choose from. This is just one of them:

Mutual Fund Screener

Criteria for High-Yield Bond Funds (Modify Screen)

Fund Availability **Only show funds available through TD AMERITRADE**	Open to New Investors **Only show funds that are open to new investors**	No Transaction Fees **Only show funds with no transaction fees**	Morningstar Category **High Yield Bond**

Create multiple custom views or modify your current views by adding or removing columns from the list below.

Select Custom View

Symbol	Name	Morningstar Category
AHYPX	American Beacon High Yld Bd Inv	High-Yield Bond
ATIPX	Aquila Three Peaks High Income I	High-Yield Bond
BJBHX	Artio Global High Income A	High-Yield Bond
BUFHX	Buffalo High-Yield	High-Yield Bond
FHYTX	Federated High-Yield	High-Yield Bond
FTYIX	Fifth Third High-Yield Bond I	High-Yield Bond
FYASX	Access Flex High-Yield Svc	High-Yield Bond
HYFIX	Harbor High-Yield Bond Inv	High-Yield Bond
JAHYX	Janus High-Yield	High-Yield Bond
LZHOX	Lazard U.S. High Yield Open	High-Yield Bond
MWHYX	Metropolitan West High Yield Bond M	High-Yield Bond
NHFIX	Northern High Yield Fixed Income	High-Yield Bond
NNHIX	Nicholas High Income N	High-Yield Bond
PAXHX	Pax World High Yield	High-Yield Bond
PHYAX	PIMCO High Yield Admin	High-Yield Bond
PHYDX	PIMCO High Yield D	High-Yield Bond
PHYRX	PIMCO High Yield R	High-Yield Bond
PYHRX	Payden High Income	High-Yield Bond
RYHGX	Rydex High Yield Strategy H	High-Yield Bond
SSHYX	SSgA High Yield Bond	High-Yield Bond
STHBX	Wells Fargo Advantage S/T Hi-Yld Bd Inv	High-Yield Bond
STHYX	Wells Fargo Advantage High Income Inv	High-Yield Bond

NAV Return (YTD)	NAV Return (1 Year)	Minimum Investment	Net Expense Ratio
+20.45%	−13.69%	$2,500	1.11%
+13.48%	−5.23%	$0	1.08%
+25.28%	−6.60%	$1,000	1.00%
+21.33%	−3.74%	$2,500	1.02%
+24.03%	−11.57%	$25,000	1.02%
+25.90%	−6.60%	$1,000	0.74%
−5.12%	−10.63%	$4,000	2.59%
+12.19%	−4.18%	$2,500	1.17%
+17.32%	−5.24%	$2,500	0.91%
+15.97%	−9.54%	$2,500	0.85%
+26.34%	−1.05%	$5,000	0.80%
+14.24%	−7.28%	$2,500	0.89%
+16.14%	−11.41%	$500	1.06%
+19.55%	−6.65%	$250	1.01%
+14.93%	−13.68%	$5,000,000	0.80%
+14.88%	−13.78%	$1,000	0.90%
+14.77%	−13.99%	$0	1.15%
+13.64%	−10.94%	$5,000	0.73%
−5.50%	−11.38%	$2,500	1.49%
+20.29%	−8.96%	$1,000	0.75%
+7.45%	−0.92%	$2,500	0.88%
+15.62%	−5.20%	$2,500	0.96%

Fund Name	Morningstar Analysis	Morningstar Category
Artio Global High Income	—	High-Yield Bond
Delaware Pooled High-Yield	—	High-Yield Bond
Harbor High-Yield Bond Ad	06-14-09	High-Yield Bond
Harbor High-Yield Bond In	06-14-09	High-Yield Bond
Harbor High-Yield Bond In	06-14-09	High-Yield Bond
Ivy High Income Y	—	High-Yield Bond
JHFunds2 U.S. High Yield	—	High-Yield Bond
JHFunds2 U.S. High Yield	—	High-Yield Bond
Loomis Sayles Instl High	—	High-Yield Bond
MainStay High Yield Corpo	6-10-09	High-Yield Bond
MEMBERS High Income A Loa	—	High-Yield Bond

Before investing in high-yield bond funds, carefully consider the security's objectives, risks, charges, and expenses.

There is a variety of ways to add a little "junk" to your trunk. But remember that high-yield bonds, unlike AAA corporate bonds, are inherently more risky than other types of credit offerings. Remember, the higher the yield, the greater the risk!

United Airlines, for instance, issued some $175 million in three-year debt at the end of June 2009. United's notes, offered with a 12.75 percent yield, were priced to yield 17 percent, as investors demanded more concessions to compensate for United's business risk.

That is the most United has paid in interest on its debt since 2000, according to Bloomberg Business News. The last time it paid even half that amount was during the last recession, and this debt offering was six full percentage points above what other airlines paid to borrow money in mid-2009.

Star Rating (%)	YTD Return (%)	Expense Ratio
★★★★★	28.85	0.75
★★★★★	28.37	0.54
★★★★★	13.88	1.02
★★★★★	14.13	0.77
★★★★★	13.84	1.14
★★★★★	25.12	1.14
★★★★★	25.95	0.82
★★★★★	25.87	0.77
★★★★★	24.46	0.72
★★★★★	22.97	1.04
★★★★★	15.0	1.0

And these are so-called senior secured notes, backed by United's collateral, which the market obviously thinks is worth less than United does. With a B+ rating, these don't qualify as junk bonds, but they are priced as if United is a bankruptcy risk.

But, assuming you choose the bonds of companies that will likely survive the recession without entering bankruptcy, or well-managed high-yield bond funds, the risk may very well be worth the reward as the economy recovers and businesses repair their stretched balance sheets.

6

HOMES, SUITES, HOMES

In 2002, I published *TrendWatching: Don't Be Fooled by the Next Investment Fad, Mania, or Bubble.*

In the wake of the stock-market crash and subsequent events of 9/11, I wanted to look back at this history of bubbles and use the accumulated wisdom of many market historians to see if I could learn enough to identify the next major speculative episode in the investment world.

The following is an excerpt from *TrendWatching* that, I believe, very accurately captures the onset of the real estate mania we have just experienced. Let's set the stage on how to profit from the end of this bubble, by purchasing distressed assets linked to soured real estate investments.

Professionals, remember, profit from the upside, the downside, and the rebound. As you will see in subsequent paragraphs discussing my record for calling turns in the markets, trust me when I say it's time for you to act like a professional here and buy back what has been sold, by others, at significant losses.

SO, WHAT'S THE NEXT BUBBLE?

If, indeed, the forces of inflation defeat the forces of deflation, or recession, which assets will likely benefit from the events that have created such expansive monetary and fiscal policies? Again, hard assets like real estate and commodities are set to benefit. Real estate has already shown a peculiar strength in an economic environment that is normally hostile to property price appreciation.

Corroborating Evidence

For the first time in modern history, housing sales and prices not only failed to weaken at any point during the recession but actually managed to advance. Such a phenomenon has never taken place in modern American economic history. Real estate mogul Sam Zell told me that in his decades as a real estate expert, he has never seen this kind of resilience during such a difficult economic period. It is true, I should note, that residential real estate is most often a lagging, rather than leading, indicator. In some cases, real estate sales and values may not decline until one or two years after the peak of an economic cycle.

In this instance, however, real estate went on to have two record-setting or near-record-setting years after the economy peaked in the fourth quarter of 1999. As a *USA Today* article suggested in mid-2002, the pace of home-price appreciation throughout the recession not only exceeded the prevailing inflation rate but expanded at a rate of 6 percent, outperforming most other asset classes in the United States. However, the recent action in home sales and housing pricing is not yet indicative of a bubble. There hasn't been the type of speculative trading of houses as there was in stocks, nor is the action yet reminiscent of the regional housing bubbles that occurred in California, New York, and Boston during the late 1980s.

Ed Yardeni, chief market strategist for Deutsche Bank Capital and a widely respected economist, makes the case that housing and housing stocks may continue to do well for quite some time despite the widely accepted view that housing activity and the appreciation in housing stocks were beginning to falter in mid-2002. Yardeni argues that with mortgage rates remaining below 7 percent, cheap by historic standards, and a record backlog of homes on order, waiting to be built, the outlook for housing remains quite strong.

Yardeni, by the way, was the first to suggest, after the stock-market bubble burst, that a housing bubble might very well be the next investment phenomenon. His view was supported by many newspaper and wire-service articles that appeared throughout the year. Some identified how hot properties in New York City, despite the lifestyle concerns created by 9/11, were still selling briskly and at above market prices.

Around the country, meanwhile, the median price for a single-family home rose to a record $147,500, up sharply from its previous high.

Surprisingly, in Silicon Valley, where the dot.com bust was felt more acutely than anywhere else in the nation, real estate prices and sales have continued to rise rapidly. Smallish Silicon Valley homes have recently sold for well over a million dollars, above their asking prices, and within only a few days of being listed.

That type of behavior is entirely anomalous given the economic circumstances that have arisen in the post–technology bubble environment.

No doubt, the run-up in real estate could very simply be the result of an extended lag time between the peak in stock prices, the economic cycle, and the expected bust in land prices. Or something entirely different and unexpected could be in the making. But it remains possible, given all the efforts undertaken by policy makers to kick-start the economy, that excess cash is now going into real estate.

The government, it seems, may be providing the necessary liquidity for a new bubble in the housing sector. Certainly, there is mounting evidence that this is the case. Investors have become so disenchanted that they are redirecting their available funds into their homes instead of stocks. Rather than gamble on Wall Street, which has been tarnished in their eyes, individuals want to bet on a sure thing.

The *New York Times* and other newspapers have suggested that investor psychology has changed dramatically as a consequence not only of the bursting of the bubble but of 9/11 and other unsettling events around the world, prompting people to reevaluate their priorities.

Home and hearth have always supported the individual investor, and hence there may be a decided shift in investor preferences. Again, this moment could signal the beginnings of a secular change in investor preferences, where hard assets—"stuff," as economic historian Jim Grant calls them—outperform financial assets for the first time in decades.

While many observers are breathlessly waiting for that new bull market in stocks to begin, a major new bull market in real estate and other hard assets may already be starting to form.

Real Benefits

In addition to the favorable macroeconomic and macro-policy influences on real estate, one must remember that it is the only investment that is heavily subsidized by the federal government.

While the bull market in stocks was raging, few individuals noticed the tax advantages of buying and holding real estate. True, home ownership reached record highs along with the stock market. But at that juncture, individuals were merely purchasing places to live, not speculating in real estate.

As investors shift their preferences, they will likely be reminded—by real estate brokers and others who stand to benefit from the coming boom—that real estate is the only investment that gives the investor a large tax break. As many know, the interest-rate deductions on a mortgage are so generous that by the time a mortgage has been fully paid, the U.S. government has picked up 40 percent of the tab.

One can make a very powerful case that the ingredients for a bull market in hard assets, particularly real estate, are present. Whether they coalesce to produce a bubble remains an open question. But a quick glance at the criteria should help clarify the situation.

So the bad news about housing is that home prices have crashed. The good news about housing is that it is now more affordable than it has been in over a generation.

The chart on the following page shows that, all things considered, housing is now the most affordable it has been since

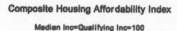

Composite Housing Affordability Index

Median Inc=Qualifying Inc=100

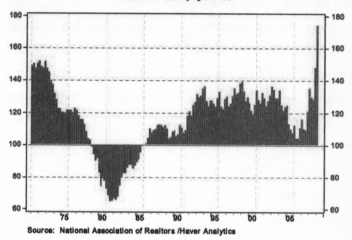

Source: National Association of Realtors /Haver Analytics

I've been on planet Earth. I still remember, fondly, the house my folks bought in suburban Buffalo, New York, when I was two years old, and where I remained until I was nearly thirteen.

The four-bedroom, one-and-a-half-bath house, with a formal dining room, family room, and small yard, totaled 2,022 square feet on a little more than a tenth of an acre. I've been back many times to see it since I moved from there in 1974, and I marvel at how the house appeared so big to me at the time. One of us got bigger, and unfortunately for me, it wasn't the house!

Still, it was a lovely new home, in a brand-new neighborhood, where I made great friends, with whom I keep in touch to this day. All the neighbors in our Italian/Polish section of town knew one another. We barbecued and played street football and made snowmen and went to school and church together. It was a community, in the truest sense of the word. And while my parents stretched, financially, to make that purchase, it turned out to be the right buy at the right time.

In that brand-new subdivision, in a town called Cheektowaga—a Native American name that means "the place of the crab apple tree"—our new house, with special storm windows included (if you ever lived in Buffalo, you know why that's necessary!), my family's piece of the American Dream cost $21,500.

Our monthly mortgage was $164.00, including taxes! On an adjusted basis, and you can choose to believe it or not, housing is as cheap today as it was back then. It is inconceivable, I know, but all the data show it's true.

The only question is whether or not you want to take advantage of a market that is as cheap now as it was when you were a baby.

I think we know what the answer *should* be. The question is whether you are prepared to make such a move and whether or not you are ready to research all the necessary information you need to begin buying assets, and not just real estate, on the cheap.

Making a move on a new, or even second, home is an important first step toward distressed investing. It would be best if we examined all the factors, from government assistance to the extremely attractive discounts around today that will help you make an informed decision about whether or not you have the foundation on which to (re)build your wealth.

A Quick Cautionary Tale

I mentioned the house we bought in Buffalo, in 1963, as a comparative note for those of you who can now afford to buy a home at 1963 prices.

I should also point out a rather critical financial mistake my family made after selling that house in 1973. We moved into 13 Creekview Drive, on November 22, 1963—the day JFK was shot and killed in Dallas. We sold the house in late 1973 and moved to Southern California on January 5, 1974. My folks made about $16,000, with the down payment returned, on the sale—a tidy sum in those days.

Given the lack of opportunity in Buffalo, my parents followed my father's family out to Los Angeles, sight unseen, to seek greater chances for gainful employment and a better life for their family.

Upon arrival, my dad looked for work, but he was offered an opportunity to buy a rather novel business from a relative of my mom's. The business was manufacturing mini–table tennis sets, which could be used by the millions of apartment dwellers in L.A. who could not fit a full-size table-tennis set into their smaller living quarters.

The tables were one-quarter the size of the regular table and had patented padded paddles so that one could play just as hard, but on a smaller surface.

My dad used the profits from the sale of our house to buy the business. He put in all the money from the house, while we rented an apartment in Northridge, California. He even enticed some old friends and neighbors to invest in this promising recreational business. We made tables and sold them to sporting goods retailers for about a year.

My older brother and I spent the summer of '74 painting the Masonite tabletops with the signature green (and probably lead-based) paint, affixing the quarter-size nets onto the aluminum frames, and reveling in the entrepreneurial effort our dad had undertaken.

Unfortunately, we had some serious setbacks along the way and ate through all of our capital. We went out of business about eighteen months later. My father filed for both business and personal bankruptcy and the down payment money we had for a house was gone. And even though both he and my mom worked for as long as they could, they never rebuilt their coffers so that they could afford their own home.

That is the main driver behind the reason I have consistently bought homes and "traded up" whenever I could. I plan on having something besides an insurance policy (and, hopefully, some nice memories) to leave my children after I move to that big housing development in the sky.

I do not mean that as a sign of disrespect to my folks. They did the best they could—they loved us, fed us, educated us, and taught us important lessons in life. It was just a mistake made out of good intentions, one that I do not wish to repeat.

Our return on investment, if you will, on the house we failed to buy would have provided a much safer return than our investment in the business. Of course, it's always easy to see that in retrospect, but you need to make your safe and sound investments first, and then move on to riskier ventures.

At the time, my dad opted for potential equity in a start-up business instead of equity in a single-family home; at the time, he could have purchased a three- or four-bedroom house, in a nice section of the San Fernando Valley, for between $35,000 and $45,000!

Had we put the $16,000 down on the house, or whatever we had left after paying off some bills and for the move, instead of into the business, it would have changed the course of our family's financial situation. A $35,000 mortgage would have cost us a few hundred dollars a month, and by today the house would be worth about ten times what we would have paid for it. The mortgage, some thirty-five years later, would have been whittled down to nothing.

We never did buy a house. We rented for the entire period after our move to California. In 1974, the rent on our first apartment was about $250 a month. Thirty-five years later, my mom's rent is about $2,000 a month, and continues to creep higher.

After a seventeen-year battle with Parkinson's disease, my dad passed away in 1996, and as I said, my mom remains a renter.

The Los Angeles real estate market has seen many severe swings in prices in the three and a half decades since my family first moved there. But regardless of the environment, whether we had purchased a home upon arrival, or after the Los Angeles real estate bubble burst in 1989, or even more recently, my parents would have been ahead of the game. Had they purchased a home instead of renting, they would have had an equity nest egg to rely on after a lifetime of hard work, on both their parts.

A home is not necessarily an investment, but it is the biggest single purchase you will ever make. And there is never a good or a bad time to buy. There are better or worse times to buy, based on market cycles, but as explained above, this is among the best times in modern history to start building equity that you'll have for your golden years.

Contrary to conventional wisdom, I don't think home equity should be used as a piggy bank to crack open every time you need some cash. You should have, if possible, and I know it's hard to do, all of the following as well:

- An emergency savings account worth six months of expenses
- Health savings accounts for the family
- Adequate life and disability insurance
- Long-term- and catastrophic-care insurance
- College savings accounts for the kids
- Retirement and pension accounts for yourself

And trust me, I get it . . . no one has all those things funded properly right now. It doesn't really matter how much you make, unless you've made a killing, you are living, saving, and spending paycheck to paycheck.

But the above items are what all the personal-finance experts say you need to have, among the five, seven, nine, or ten steps toward reaching wealth, riches, financial security, blah, blah, blah. And they add that you should pay off your high-cost credit-card debt.

Really? I realize that if you could, you would.

Just as an aside, I think that almost all of the personal-finance "gurus"—with the exception of Jane Bryant Quinn and Jean Chatzky—are utterly and completely "FoS," and I don't mean "friends of Streisand."

They, arguably, give you the emotional tools to tackle your financial problems but very few financial tools with which to make money. If you can't balance a checkbook by now, you have more than just financial troubles, it seems to me.

There are no simple ten-step programs for prosperity, you're not poor because you want to be, nor is there "a secret" to success. Personally, I believe Steve Martin gave the best piece of personal finance advice ever: If you want to be a millionaire, start by getting a million dollars!

But building long-term equity in a home gives you peace of mind that when you're retiring, your monthly nut will be considerably smaller if you own a home, outright, than if you still have to pay the landlord. And it is just one piece of a financial puzzle you need to put in place in order to build long-term wealth and security.

Still, what I am about to say requires a huge leap of faith, given our recent experiences:

The risk right now isn't buying real estate. The real risk is NOT buying it, particularly at such depressed prices.

This advice is clearly more applicable to first-time buyers and retirees, both of whom may not be saddled with homes they can't sell or underwater mortgages, or who may lack the ability to obtain financing for a home purchase.

However, it also applies to anyone whose mortgage is not underwater, and who has ample cash and a strong credit rating, and who wants to make a move.

Ninety percent of Americans are still employed. There is a once-in-a-generation opportunity in real estate to find real and historic bargains in the market.

I will show you a few of the countless examples of quality discounted real estate that is available virtually anywhere in the country. It is also true that in other countries of the world, such as Spain, Italy, France, Greece, Ireland, and England, to name but a few, similar bargains abound.

This is not a rich person's guide to real estate. This section is for anyone who missed out during the greatest real estate bubble in history, avoided the pitfalls of exotic mortgages, and can now buy a dream house for a dream price.

You may doubt me. But don't! Had you bought a home in 2005, using creative financing and little money down, you would have paid a much steeper price than you will pay today.

As a place to hang your hat, as an investment, as a tax break, and as future security, a house today is not just a home; it is, again, one of several necessary nest eggs to sit alongside your other household assets.

Getting Started

There is no better time to get started investing in real estate than right now. In addition to the depressed prices for new, single-family homes, condos, apartment buildings, and vacation properties, there is a variety of new government programs designed to put a floor under falling home prices and help you buy a house.

First of all, through the remainder of 2009, all first-time home buyers are entitled to a refundable $8,000 tax credit on the purchase of a home.

There is also a bill pending in the Senate that would nearly double the tax credit to $15,000 and make it available to anyone who buys a home, not just first-time buyers.

Despite the tightening of lending standards among the nation's cash-strapped banks, there are plenty of willing lenders, as well as government assistance, to get you into a home. That assumes, of course, that you are not bankrupt, and that you have decent credit, an appropriate down payment, and a job.

To be frank, the days of so-called liar or NINJA loans discussed earlier are over.

(There are still some con artists out there trying to lure home buyers into very bad deals, so it is still a "buyer beware" market in mortgages! In fact, the government is actively seeking out the scammers to avoid a repeat of recent problems.)

And, by the way, should you obtain financing to buy a home anytime soon, use a conventional, thirty-year, fixed-rate mortgage. These rates are as low as you will ever see them in your lifetime.

The Federal Reserve, when it was desperately trying to prevent a collapse of the financial system, and a depression, last year, cut short-term interest rates to zero. They can't go any lower than that.

Mortgage rates between 4.75 percent and 6 percent are historically low. Absolutely do NOT make the mistake that home buyers made in 2005, 2006, and 2007, when they took out adjustable and/or exotic "pay-option ARMS," which allowed you to drive your monthly mortgage payment to a bedrock rate, through financial engineering.

Prices have collapsed on the homes themselves! Do not get greedy, or sloppy, by falling for any come-ons that suggest you lower your monthly payment further with an adjustable-rate loan whose monthly payments, at this juncture in history, are as low as they'll ever be—and have nowhere to go but up from here!

The Foundation You Need

Before we explore the various opportunities that are government financed, let's define some terms so you will know how this game works right now.

- There are many ways to purchase distressed real estate. You can simply buy homes in any one of the locations I mentioned previously, where prices have plunged over the last two years, using conventional means.

- You can buy a house out of foreclosure, either from a bank, or some government entity.

- You can purchase a house that is being "sold short" by the owner or a bank. In a short sale, the home seller, or the bank, takes whatever price the market will bear, despite what is owed on the mortgage. The bank agrees to the market price and forgives the rest of the debt. This is a relatively new practice that occurred during this last real estate bust. It gets the seller out of a house he or she cannot afford, damages his or her credit less than a foreclosure, and prevents the bank from taking the keys and having to carry the house as a loss on its books. It is not an entirely win-win scenario, but it beats the alternative.

- You can invest in real estate investment trusts (REITS) or other investment funds that buy residential real estate. Many have raised billions of dollars in capital to buy distressed real estate. I'll talk more about those later in the book.

The Old-Fashioned Way

At this juncture, the simplest way to do that is to find a reasonably priced home that fits the Fannie Mae– or Freddie Mac– conforming mortgage requirements, a home priced between $417,000 and $625,000—depending on whether you live in an "average" neighborhood or a "high cost" area of the country.

If you live in Alaska, Hawaii, Guam, or the U.S. Virgin Islands, the loan limit could reach as high as $721,050. Don't ask me why they threw in the extra fifty bucks on the last one. . . . I'm sure that in Hawaii that extra $50 goes a long, long way to getting you waterfront property!

You are typically required to put 20 percent down and have a solid FICO, or credit, score to qualify for a conforming loan.

With an FHA loan, however, you can put down as little as 3.5 percent, use money "gifted" from a family member or friend as the down payment, and use the current $8,000 tax credit toward the down payment as well.

(If the government extends the tax credit beyond 2009 and raises it to $15,000 for all home buyers, as I mentioned earlier, the same would likely be true under those circumstances as well.)

Home builder Lennar, which is offering 4 percent mortgages, explains very clearly how the first-time home-buyer tax credits can be useful, well into 2010.

First-Time Home-Buyer Tax Credit
Quick Facts and 2008 Tax-Refund Opportunities

- An $8,000 tax credit is available for first-time home buyers.
- A first-time home buyer is defined as someone who has not owned a principal residence during the three years prior to the purchase.
- This tax credit does not have to be repaid as did the

previous tax credit, if the property is held for a minimum of three years.

- The tax credit is available for homes closed on or after January 1, 2009, and on or before November 30, 2009.
- You can take advantage of the tax credit relative to your 2008 tax year.
- The tax credit can be applied against your 2008 tax return, which is generally filed on or before April 15, 2009.
- If you have already filed your 2008 tax return, you can immediately amend your return once you purchase a home, and you should receive a refund in thirty to sixty days.
- You should consult with a tax professional to determine how best to take advantage of the tax credit relative to your personal situation.

FHA financing ONLY: if you received or are planning to receive a loan from a family member to use toward the down payment of your home, the refund you may receive as a result of the tax credit can assist you in buying a home.

Fannie Mae and Freddie Mac, the now-nationalized "government-sponsored enterprises" (GSEs), are among the institutions that help lenders and borrowers provide and obtain mortgages at more affordable rates than they would typically be able to access in the private market.

Fannie and Freddie are also making a move toward helping existing home owners refinance mortgages that are as much as 25 percent underwater, meaning that the home is worth that much less than the existing mortgage. That could be a very big help to the housing market, and would have a carryover effect in aiding the market for new and existing home sales as well.

From there, the process is a normal one of picking out a house, obtaining a mortgage, closing the deal, and moving in. Other methods of buying distressed real estate include options that have arisen just recently in this real estate recession.

They include purchasing a house in foreclosure, buying a house that is being "sold short" by the owner, buying a house directly from a bank (bank-owned sale), or buying properties that are in the hands of the federal government.

You would be quite surprised to see just how active the federal government is in auctioning off foreclosed and IRS-seized properties. Property seizures are usually the result of unpaid back taxes or the confiscation of assets from convicted criminals (oh, if those walls could talk!).

As for government assistance, let me show you a couple of things that might very well open your eyes to the number of programs in place at various government agencies, which are offering you important assistance in buying a home.

(Just a note: There are also assistance programs designed to keep home owners in their houses through foreclosure mitigation. Anyone facing foreclosure should go to the Housing and Urban Development, Treasury, or FHA Web sites for further guidance and help.)

Buy or Build?

The number of unoccupied homes in the United States reached 19.1 million in the first quarter of 2009 and is likely to keep rising as the real estate recession wears on.

Almost 20 million homes unoccupied! Out of the 130.4 million homes in the United States, 2.1 million empty properties were for sale, 4.2 million unoccupied homes were for rent, and 4.9 million vacation homes stood vacant, according to Census Bureau data quoted by Bloomberg News. The rest included foreclosures.

That is an extraordinary supply of homes waiting for buyers willing to step up and take advantage of the glut of properties around the country. Many of those homes are brand, spanking new in developments that the big home builders put in place at the peak of the housing frenzy. From new homes in Henderson, Nevada, to ocean-front high-rises in Miami, there is no shortage of homes, which means no shortage of opportunities in real estate!

Indeed, the government, through various programs, is also making it easier to acquire condominiums, given the enormous numbers of condos for sale. As noted in the *Wall Street Journal*, below:

CONDOS VIE FOR THE GOOD HOUSE-LENDING SEAL OF APPROVAL AS SALES SLUMP, DEVELOPERS TOUT BACKING FROM FHA, WHICH HELPS BUYERS QUALIFY FOR LOWER DOWN PAYMENTS

■

BY NICK TIMIRAOS

June 17, 2009 | A nationwide glut of new condominiums has prompted developers to use new marketing ploys to sell their units. One increasingly popular move: get a government stamp of approval for the entire building. The approval, from the Federal Housing Administration, means potential buyers can more easily qualify for a low-down-payment mortgage backed by the FHA—a highly coveted amenity in this era of tight credit.

With a little research on the Web, you can find sites that will take you to exactly the community you'd like to explore and show you the prices and deals on newly developed homes.

For instance, American Home Guides provides a look at homes available in Southern California, just north of Los Angeles.

Many of the builders of new communities also provide incentives, including below-market mortgage rates and cash rebates. This type of activity is going on all across the country. You can see, on their various Web sites, in California alone, there are numerous ways to purchase new homes at very affordable rates.

I plugged in a price range of $175,000 to $300,000 to get a list of homes shown as an example of what's available in a single zip code. The list was long and impressive.

Among the nation's most prominent builders are the Ryland Group, Hovnanian, Toll Brothers, Pulte Homes, Centex, and D.R. Horton.

I am, by no means, being compensated by any builder to show their homes, nor do I have business relationships with mortgage brokers, lenders, or real estate firms.

What I am trying to show you is that with a little work, it's pretty simple to use the Web to scout out sites that just might have the right home for you, at the right price.

You need not go any further than the newspapers, be they local or national, to find opportunity knocking on your door.

In a fascinating story, published by the *Wall Street Journal* on July 6, 2009, immediately after Independence Day, the original buyers of the $8.4 billion City Center Condominium project in Las Vegas, one of the hardest-hit real estate markets in the country, were said to be in open revolt, demanding that MGM Mirage and Dubai World, the developers, offer "significant price reductions" on contracts they had already signed!

There are, the *Journal* reported, deposits on 1,500 units, totaling $313 million, most of which were purchased during the boom years of 2006 and 2007. The *Journal* said buyers are taking their battle to the Web . . . via a protest page . . . www.citycentercondodeposit.blogspot.com.

While Iranians are using the Web to launch the "green revolution" to revolt against a repressive regime, the restive natives of Sin City are trying to topple not a government, but Arab and American luxury-condo developers! The world's ironies never cease.

This is shaping up to be a major legal battle that could end up either setting a floor, or a ceiling, for condo prices in a city and state with the highest foreclosure rate in the nation.

Still, after nearly going bankrupt, City Center has significant challenges, which could end up benefiting you. There are still condos for sale, and if the current occupants have their way, already-purchased condos will be reduced in price, which will force down the price of unsold units.

This is the type of work you need to do, the kind of awareness you need to have, to profit during times of market turbulence.

Admittedly, the distressed property you ultimately buy may not be the mansion of your wildest dreams, but the home will likely be brand-new, affordable, and part of a desirable community.

That is the definition of the American Dream when it comes to home ownership. Our recent lust for real estate led us to a point where everyone believed an 8,000-square-foot McMansion was the norm and no longer the exception.

Home ownership, whether the home is a million-dollar mansion for the well-off, or something more affordably priced for most of us, provides shelter, security, equity, tax breaks, and a way of life to which we all aspire.

For Sale or Fore-Closure? The Real Opportunity in Real Estate

For the individual investor, there is simply no need to chase extremely esoteric or incomprehensible investments to make money by investing in distressed assets.

We can start right where the recent problem began, with the bursting of the real estate bubble, leading to massive fore-closures on everything from sub-prime homes to extra-prime luxury homes. Single-family homes, condos, co-ops, vacation homes, and investment properties all have plunged in value since the peak in real estate prices, four years ago.

Hard to believe, isn't it? Real estate, nationally, topped out in price somewhere between 2006 and 2007, depending on where you live, and here we are in 2009, still thinking that the bubble has just burst. Seems like only yesterday, the equity in our homes was making us a fortune, doesn't it?

According to the most trusted source on housing prices these days, Professor Robert Shiller of Yale University, home prices, according to the index he and a partner put together, the S&P/Case-Shiller Home Price Indices, shows that housing prices, nationally, have declined almost 20 percent from their highs. Other data from Case-Shiller's 20-City Composite show an even steeper decline of about 32 percent!

In June 2009, a Deutsche Bank analyst predicted that prices had another 14 percent to fall before bottoming out. That means a couple of things: First, that housing could still get worse before it gets better, as could the economy. But it also means that you have plenty of time to go looking for deals in housing, at bargain-basement prices.

According to the National Association of Realtors, the median price of a new home, across the United States, in the second quarter of 2009, was $169,000, down from a peak of nearly $222,000 in 2006. That's a 24 percent discount on a home.

If you were to buy a median-priced home, at $169,000, out of foreclosure with an FHA loan, you would require a down payment of less than $6,000, which the government's refundable tax credit would more than cover, leaving you a further $2,000 benefit from Uncle Sam.

Nevada, for instance, the home of Sin City, has the highest

foreclosure rate in the nation. In Phoenix, the average price of a home has plunged about 50 percent. That's right—50 percent! Phoenix is having a "half-off" sale on housing.

Let's look at all of the factors involved in buying foreclosed real estate today.

As recently as May 2009, foreclosures were 18 percent above year-earlier levels, according to RealtyTrac, which follows national and statewide foreclosures. According to the service, 1 in every 398 homes received a foreclosure notice in May, as bankers came calling in record numbers.

Pick your spot, but as you can see, everywhere in the nation, the foreclosure phenomenon is a powerful force in real estate.

Las Vegas has the nation's highest foreclosure rate, while California and Florida ran a close second and third. According to RealtyTrac, ten states accounted for 77 percent of the total number of foreclosures and defaults, many of these states being quite desirable and, of course, recently among the priciest destinations.

RealtyTrac even offers a course in buying foreclosed real estate and negotiating short sales with banks!

Foreclosures are at record numbers, one out of every six U.S. homes is upside down, government bailout . . . What does this mean to you? Do you realize how all the recent actions and conditions are creating an opportunity for

millions to be made, not by just savvy investors but by anyone who really knows how to approach this industry the right way?

The question is . . . Are you going to take action and capture a piece of the pie for yourself?

If so, then we can show the exact steps to take to make it happen!

TCS Foreclosures, the advanced foreclosure training partner of RealtyTrac, has a proprietary system that is creating fortunes for those involved. Because of all the recent problems in the housing market, the TCS system—the only one in the nation providing this service—has been achieving amazing results.

Our system, which took over nine years to develop, just happens to be exactly what the lenders in regards to the government are looking for. And our clients are making all kinds of money in the process. We are fortunate to be the only company doing it, and that puts our clientele into an elite group of probably less than 1 percent of everyone trying to capitalize from the foreclosure industry.

—*Patrick Grom*
Director of Training, TCS Foreclosures

Admittedly, it's not that easy to pack up all your troubles in your old kit bag and smile, smile, smile . . . *and* make a major move. But considering that no one's current situation is all that secure, buying a house on the cheap, in one of the country's most pleasant, sunny, and reasonably good economies is worth a look.

Some of the opportunities on foreclosures are simply eye-popping. (Again these are dated and for illustrative purposes only. But as time wears on, and as long as unemployment hovers near twenty-six-year highs, foreclosure sales, unfortunately, will remain ample.) Look at some of these listings on page 164, from the Web site foreclosure.com.

While I don't recommend bidding on properties sight unseen, foreclosure.com has rather extensive data on locations, aerial photos of the properties and neighborhoods, and many other details that make a long-distance and online pur-chase the "next best thing to being there," as AT&T used to say.

Still, there is no substitute for making the trip to a destina-tion that interests you and exploring the city, the neighbor-hood, and the property that might elicit a bid.

And this is just one page from many different and helpful real estate sites, outlining the thousands of opportunities, in the Miami area alone, that deal with foreclosed properties.

I have a little joke I use at public speaking engagements, about how if you live in the tristate area of New York, New Jersey, and Connecticut, by law, you MUST move to Florida by age sixty.

The Sunshine State is, effectively, a retirement commu-nity for northeasterners who, every winter, or in the winter of their lives, flock to Florida to escape the cold, and bask in the golden rays that accompany the golden years.

The good news is that there has never been a better time to fly south for the winter!

During the real estate boom in Florida, particularly in Miami, builders went nuts. Despite the fact that the highest number of condominiums sold in any given year in Miami's recent history was 8,000 and the average number of sales totaled 5,000 per year, Miami developers added between 80,000 and 90,000 condos to Miami's housing supply during the boom years!

#	Listing Type	City	ST
1	QuickSale℠	Miami	FL
2	QuickSale℠	Miami	FL
3	QuickSale℠	Miami Beach	FL
4	QuickSale℠	Miami	FL
5	QuickSale℠	Miami	FL
6	QuickSale℠	Hialeah	FL
7	Foreclosure	Miami	FL
8	Foreclosure	Hialeah	FL
9	Foreclosure	Miami	FL
10	Foreclosure	Miami	FL
11	Foreclosure	Miami	FL
12	Foreclosure	Miami	FL
13	Foreclosure	Homestead	FL
14	Foreclosure	Hialeah	FL
15	Foreclosure	Miami	FL
16	Foreclosure	North Miami	FL
17	Foreclosure	Miami	FL
18	Foreclosure	Miami	FL
19	Foreclosure	Miami	FL
20	Foreclosure	North Miami	FL
21	Foreclosure	Miami Beach	FL
22	Foreclosure	Opa Locka	FL
23	Foreclosure	Miami	FL
24	Foreclosure	Miami	FL
25	Foreclosure	Miami	FL

That's almost twenty years' worth of sales. The glut of building left many developments unoccupied, underoccupied, converted to rentals, bankrupt, or repossessed by banks.

The condos are being sold at fire-sale prices, as the foreclosure.com page shows. The same is true for single-family homes in Miami, and from northern to southern Florida.

There are huge foreclosure sales in Henderson, Nevada, just outside of Las Vegas; in Southern California, from San

Zip	BD/BH	Price	Zestimate®
33180	2 / 2	$400,000	
33157	5 / 3	$350,000	
33141	1 / 1	$169,900	
33147	6 / 5	$200,000	
33168	3 / 2	$129,000	$210,500
33014	1 / 1	$199,500	$357,500
33165	3 / 3	$220,900	$277,000
33015	3 / 2	$143,900	$202,000
33150	3 / 2	$25,900	$205,000
33161	2 / 1	$89,000	$190,000
33193		$105,000	
33138	2 / 2	$155,000	$256,500
33033	4 / 2	$138,900	$301,500
33015	2 / 2	$52,000	$154,000
33161	2 / 2	$85,000	$175,500
33160	2 / 2	$62,900	$219,000
33177	3 / 3	$153,900	$222,500
33138	1 / 1	$92,900	$152,000
33144	3 / 2	$159,000	$274,500
33160		$108,000	
33140	4 / 4	$474,000	$1,242,000
33055	3 / 2	$131,900	$223,500
33189	4 / 2	$148,900	
33133	2 / 2	$82,000	$171,000
33131		$181,500	

Diego to the so-called Inland Empire, about an hour east of L.A.; and across the rest of the country.

FYI, foreclosure.com is a subscription site. But there are free sites, such as Realtor.com and condo.com, that also are useful in locating bargains, foreclosures, and other opportunities in both residential and commercial real estate.

One very interesting company focusing on foreclosures is Gorilla Capital. It is, essentially, one-stop shopping for individuals who do not want to do their own research but would rather rely on a service to find foreclosed properties that meet their needs and their price points.

Check out the company's way of doing business. They currently operate in Oregon and Arizona. But they are planning to expand around the United States. Gorilla sends out e-mail alerts with monthly foreclosure reports.

With the advent of the Internet and other technological advances, real estate is becoming less regional, allowing buyers to seek out properties online before expending the time, energy, and cash to make a move to locations that are better suited to their financial situations.

Gorilla focuses on affordable foreclosures in the $100,000–$180,000 range, the sweet spot of the most affordable homes, and also offers easier financing options and more government assistance than are available at significantly higher price points.

Gorilla shows the listings and offers homes for sale on the Internet. It doesn't get much easier than this. I am not endorsing Gorilla, but I should add that all the various government assistance programs, from the VA to the FHA to the USDA (Department of Agriculture), can be used to purchase foreclosed properties from Gorilla.

Meantime, for those of you interested in foreclosed properties, let's look at a few Web pages, just to get an idea of what Uncle Sam has to offer:

Homes for Sale by the U.S. Government

The HomeSales.gov Web site provides current information about single-family homes for sale by the U.S. federal government. These previously owned homes are for sale by public auction or other methods, depending on the property. Anyone can buy a home for sale by the U.S. government, but you must work with a real estate agent, broker, or servicing representative to submit an offer or bid.

Currently the U.S. Departments of Housing and Urban Development (HUD), Agriculture (USDA/Rural Development), and Veterans Affairs (VA) have homes listed on this site. For additional information regarding property listings, please contact the corresponding agency.

Or how about this, from the U.S. Treasury Department?

JUNE 2009 AUCTIONS

SINGLE FAMILY HOME: 320 Westmoor Drive,
White Hall, Illinois 62092

ON-LINE AUCTION DATES: June 10–19, 2009

Auction Extended One Week!

NEW LOWER STARTING BID! 1,662 ± sq. ft.
one-level home with 3 bedrooms, 2 baths, living
room with fireplace, and attached 2-car garage.
Sale # 09-66-893.

SINGLE FAMILY HOME: 3945 Dayton Xenia Road,
Beavercreek, Ohio 45432

ON-LINE AUCTION DATES: June 10–12, 2009

1,059 ± sq. ft. one-level home with 3 bedrooms,
1 bath, living room with fireplace, deck, and
detached garage. Located in the community of
North Beavercreek. Sale # 09-66-825.

SINGLE FAMILY HOME: 1119 Windmere Way, Allen,
Texas 75013

AUCTION DATE: Tuesday, June 16, 2009

4,174 ± sq. ft. home with 4 bedrooms, 3.5 baths,
2nd-floor media and rec rooms, in-ground pool,
and attached 3-car garage. Located in Waterford
Crossing. Sale # 09-66-166.

SINGLE FAMILY HOME: 6408 N. Queensway Drive,
Temple Terrace, Florida 33617

AUCTION DATE: Wednesday, June 17, 2009

2,383 ± sq. ft. one-level home with 4 bedrooms,
2.5 baths, fireplace, screened porch, and attached
2-car garage. Located in an established neighbor-
hood near Tampa. Sale # 09-66-150.

SINGLE FAMILY HOME: 111 Rincon Drive, Del Rio,
Texas 78840

AUCTION DATE: Wednesday, June 17, 2009

4,318 ± sq. ft. one-level home with 4 bedrooms,
3.5 baths, 2 fireplaces, patio, and attached 3-car
garage. Located in the South Del Rio neighbor-
hood. Sale # 09-66-169.

SINGLE FAMILY HOME: RR5, Box 3799, Mile 9 Road N,
Mercedes, Texas 78570

AUCTION DATE: Thursday, June 18, 2009

2,085 ± sq. ft. one-level home with 3 bedrooms, 2
baths, covered patio, and attached 2-car garage.
The home is located on a 4.91 ± acre lot in Cam-
pacuas. Sale # 09-66-122.

SINGLE FAMILY HOME: 1216 Harvey Street, McAllen,
Texas 78501

AUCTION DATE: Thursday, June 18, 2009

1,559 ± sq. ft. one-level home with 2 bedrooms,

2 baths, covered porch, and attached 2-car

garage. The home is located in West Highland.

Sale # 09-66-132.

SINGLE FAMILY HOME: 6124 Mary Lane Drive,

San Diego, California 92115

AUCTION DATE: Thursday, June 25, 2009

1,405 ± sq. ft. one-level home with 3 bedrooms,

2 baths, fireplace, patio, and attached 2-car garage.

Near the campus of SDSU. Sale # 09-66-891.

While dated, these examples are for illustration purposes only, and should give you a good idea of what's available through the government's auction process.

(I never realized it, either, by the way, but the USDA offers financial assistance to would-be homeowners in rural communities and sells homes, ranches, and farms around the country, both directly and in sealed-bid auctions! Its Web site is www.usda.gov.)

Do-It-Yourself Distressed

There are even new exchanges that allow individuals, and professionals, to buy distressed mortgages on their own. THIS is a risky game for novices, but if you have experience in the sector, it's possible that you are well informed enough to buy and sell mortgage-backed securities. It involves a great deal of homework to understand the "vintages," geographical composition, gender mix, and credit and interest-rate risks associated with these securities.

DebtX, TheDebtExchange (www.debtx.com), is an exchange through which troubled loans are bought and sold by investors.

The *New York Times* highlighted the rise of these new online sites in late April 2009. Other sites such as www .loanmarket.net and www.bigbidder.com allow you to buy distressed residential mortgage notes, some of which offer extremely attractive yields.

From loanmarket.net:

STATE: Louisiana
LISTING PRICE: $100,000
LIEN POSITION: 1st
LTV: 65.02%
NOTE RATE: 9.25%

STATE: California
LISTING PRICE: $503,569
LIEN POSITION: 1st
LTV: 33.48%
NOTE RATE: 12.25%

And check this out. . . . You can buy first and second mortgages on homes right off the Web . . . in what appears to be a highly robust market for selling private mortgages. This is, quite obviously, more of a speculation than a safe investment, but it is representative of what's happening in the mortgage marketplace and how rapidly it is evolving through technological innovation.

I would also suggest you check out bigbidder.com for live bidding on first- and second-mortgage notes. You can bid online for notes with very attractive yields. Again, this requires some homework, but the availability of these new tools gives individuals a chance to take advantage of the post-crash opportunities that were recently available only to the pros.

Get Away for Less

Not surprisingly, vacation-home values continue to drop in the nation's getaway spots. Most striking was the reported drop in home sales in New York's ultra-fancy Hamptons, an exclusive enclave on the far end of Long Island.

In the first quarter of 2009, home sales in the Hamptons, where hedge-fund managers, movie moguls, and stars mingle on their high-priced estates, fell by a whopping 68 percent, the largest drop since 1982, when records were first kept on area home sales.

Even more stunning than the houses themselves, *Town & Country* reported that the median sale price of a Hamptons home fell by 28 percent, to less than $700,000, while the total value of sales in the area plummeted by 78 percent to $140.2 million!

No doubt, Nantucket, Martha's Vineyard, Aspen, and other hot spots for the jet set are faring just as poorly.

Not surprisingly, all this has put downward pressure on vacation rental prices in many of the most desirable destinations around the country.

So as far as real estate is concerned, it's not just a buyer's market, it's a renter's market as well.

And it's not just the laps of luxury that are seeing prices fall.

The downturn will also affect time-shares, both for affordable and luxury deals. Time-share prices are falling as cash-strapped consumers pull back on discretionary outlays of any kind.

SellMyTimeshareNOW.com appears to have homed in on the deeply discounted market, with sales on a one-bedroom unit in Los Cabos, Mexico, quoted at $11,995 for one week per year.

(Los Cabos, incidentally, is one of my favorite places, and one of the most beautiful resort cities on the planet. But recent drug-related violence across Mexico has made various parts of the Latin American nation a less desirable location.

From Cabo San Lucas to the boardwalk of Atlantic City to the Green Mountains of Vermont, it appears buyers have an edge here, as well. From buying new time-shares to resales, supplies are plentiful, if time-shares are part of your vacation style.

7

THE REALLY BIG BAILOUT

TAF, TARP, TALF, PDCF, AMLF, CPFF,
MMIFF, and PPIP

IN ALL MY DAYS AS A FINANCIAL JOURNALIST AND MONEY MAN-
ager, I have never seen such a glut of acronyms to describe
the myriad programs devised by the federal government to
absorb or support the mountains of bad debts accumulated
by U.S. financial institutions.

Each program, which I will not fully describe here, was
put in place by either the Federal Reserve or the U.S. Treasury to deal with the variety of troubles that befell banks, brokers, insurance companies, and other businesses that were
sorely in need of cash, financial guarantees, or other kinds of
support.

These programs, which ran into the trillions of dollars, put out a lifeline to the likes of Citigroup, AIG, Bank of America, and a host of smaller but consequential institutions whose failure could have jeopardized the entire system.

A couple of these programs will actually serve to benefit investors directly, which I will now discuss. For those of you who find it hard to sleep at night, I recommend heading to www.federalreserve.gov to read about all the lending facilities, which are discussed in painstaking detail.

For the record, I actually find it fascinating reading, but it is utterly incomprehensible to folks who do not spend a lifetime deciphering "Fedspeak."

The Fed has a language all its own, and unfortunately, the folks over at Rosetta Stone have yet to create a program to help laypeople understand what the hell the Fed is talking about.

In case you don't believe me, here's an explanation of the Fed's ABCPMMMFLF: from www.federalreserve.gov.

ASSET-BACKED COMMERCIAL PAPER
MONEY MARKET MUTUAL FUND
LIQUIDITY FACILITY

The Asset-Backed Commercial Paper Money Market Mutual Fund Liquidity Facility (AMLF) is a lending facility that finances the purchases of high-quality asset-backed commercial paper (ABCP) from money market mutual funds by U.S. depository institutions and bank holding companies. The program is intended to assist money funds that hold such paper to meet the demands for redemptions by investors and to foster liquidity in the ABCP market and money markets more generally. Collateral policies for the AMLF are discussed in the collateral and rate setting and risk management sections of this website. The loans extended through the AMLF are non-recourse loans, meaning that the borrower's obligation to repay the loan can be fulfilled by surrendering the collateral. To help ensure that the AMLF is used for its intended purpose of providing a temporary liquidity backstop to money market mutual funds (MMMFs), the Federal Reserve has established a redemption threshold whereby a MMMF must experience material outflows—defined as at least 5% of net assets in a single day or at least 10% of net assets within the prior five business days—before it can sell asset-backed commercial paper (ABCP) that would be eligible collateral for AMLF loans to depository institutions and bank holding companies. Any eligible ABCP purchased from a MMMF that has experienced redemptions at these thresholds could be pledged to AMLF at any time within the five business days following the date that the threshold level of redemptions was reached. The terms and conditions of the facility and other information are presented on this website.

Believe it or not, despite the rather arcane nature of the material, these are extremely vital programs that were put in place by the Fed at the height of the credit crisis, and were it not for these programs, I would not be writing a book discussing opportunities in distressed investments, I'd be writing a book about finding a safe cave in which to raise your family!

But two programs, the TALF and PPIP, specifically, are of more interest to the individual investor. These plans will assist large institutions in buying the so-called toxic debt from troubled banks around the country. In turn, the financial firms will create investment funds so that the individual investor can participate in these bailout programs. As a result, balance sheets of troubled banks will become healthier, so that they can start lending again.

The Treasury has chosen nine different financial firms, from BlackRock to Wellington to Invesco to Marathon Asset Management, to participate in the PPIP program. Initially, the government and these private institutions will use about $40 billion to buy troubled assets. If successful, it may grow to about three times that size.

While it was initially expected that the two programs would create trillions of dollars' worth of pooled investment opportunities, which could take the form of mutual funds, the efforts have been scaled back, of late.

Marked improvements in the financial markets made banks a bit reluctant to sell the loans at deep discounts. With markets improving, banks themselves were buying some of their own toxic assets and taking advantage of sky-high rates of return. It's hard to know if regulators will let this continue, since the very investments they are buying back are the same investments that got them in trouble in the first place!

Still, as the real estate cycle shifts from souring residential real estate loans to souring credit-card loans, student loans, SBA loans, and commercial real estate loans, the TALF, or Term Asset-Backed Securities Loan Facility, will be used by big investors to purchase securities that are backed by all those types of credit and resell them to investors . . . or . . . YOU!

You can be among the buyers of distressed asset-backed securities, or ABS, as they are called on Wall Street, and profit from the forced sale of these distressed securities.

You will see these take the form of mutual funds, as I said, and they will be aggressively marketed in the relatively near future.

Similarly, the Public-Private Investment Program, PPIP, will help banks rid themselves of bad real estate loans, from sub-prime loans to other troubled assets.

The program, envisioned to be a $1 trillion behemoth, will begin at $20 billion and, quite possibly, get bigger. And, again, you can expect Invesco, BlackRock, and others to repackage and sell the distressed assets as mutual funds.

The public may very well play an important role, not only bailing out but also profiting from the bailout of the nation's financial industry. If true, it would, essentially, be the first time in history that the post-bubble playing field would be somewhat level for professionals and individuals alike.

EPILOGUE

HAVING OFFERED A SPECIFIC VIEW ON THE COMING BUBBLE in hard assets, in general, and real estate, in particular, some seven years ago, I have not at all changed my thinking about speculative episodes with the passage of time. As was the main thesis in *TrendWatching*, the fruits of the coming bubble, investment fad, or mania are sewn into the efforts to counteract the effects of the bubble just burst!

Distressed investing is the fad of this cycle. However, in many ways, it is far more than that, even though "distressed" is *in* on Wall Street right now.

This is a long-term opportunity to rebuild wealth and take advantage of market dislocations that have unfairly punished asset prices, as if each home, stock, bond, or other investment is exactly the same as the next.

At the height of the crisis, the selling was indiscriminate and the baby, most often, was thrown out with the bathwater, particularly with respect to real estate that has collapsed in value, stocks that are trading at historically low valuations, or credit instruments that offer generous yields with the prospect of full recovery for the borrower.

This is more than a fad, it's a true opportunity. Now is the time to pick up the pieces and get back into the markets.

Crashes and crises create value in the markets, just as much as they destroy. This is a golden opportunity for those who shepherded cash during the boom times to once again go against the crowd and buy what others are still selling or afraid to buy, as I have stressed over and over again.

First-time home buyers, long-term investors, and individuals who want to add some risk to their portfolios should be running toward Main Street real estate and Wall Street stocks, even while most others are fleeing the markets.

It is my hope that this new book will help you accomplish exactly that, based on the time-tested principles of my previous works.

A final thought to leave you with, lest you think we are alone in our troubles.

On July 9, 2009, the *Wall Street Journal* chronicled the woes of a mining town in West Africa that went bust when

Huts like these were hit by a glut in Nionsomoridou, Guinea,
after residents added accommodations for mine workers
who have since left.

commodity prices crashed at the height of the credit and financial market crisis.

As the *Journal* put it, there was a "hut glut" in the village you see above, as work dried up and residents walked away from their newly constructed homes.

You may not think about it much, but the real estate bust was a global phenomenon, affecting everyone from Manhattan to Miami, from Michigan to Moscow, and from Nevada to Nionsomoridou.

Booms and busts are frequently not just local events. And we can trust that no matter where we are in time, or geography, another boom will follow this bust, as sure as night follows day.

INDEX

CREDITS AND PERMISSIONS

p. 11 "Some See an Economy in Crisis, but the Intrepid Find Bargains." From *The New York Times*, © May 29, 2009, *The New York Times*, all rights reserved. Used by permission and protected by the Copyright Laws of the United States. The printing, copying, redistribution, or retransmission of the Material without express written permission is prohibited.

p. 101 "But I see inflation as the greater future challenge . . ." from *The Financial Times*, © June 26, 2009.

p. 155 "Condos Vie for the Good House-Lending Seal of Approval," from *The Wall Street Journal*, June 17, 2009. Reprinted by permission of "How to Make a Fortune from the Biggest Bailout in U.S. History," copyright © 2009 Dow Jones & Company, Inc. All Rights Reserved Worldwide. License number 2256011194764.

p. 161 Realty Trac/TCS Foreclosures, courtesy Patrick Grom, TCS Foreclosures.

p. 167 Home Sales, courtesy U.S. Department of the Treasury.

p. 167 Seized Real Property Public Auctions, courtesy U.S. Department of the Treasury.

p. 171 Louisiana house listing and photo, courtesy LoanMarket, Inc.

p. 171 California house listing and photo, courtesy LoanMarket, Inc.

pp. 182–83 "A Housing Market Built on Mud Takes Off, and Then Goes Thud," from *The Wall Street Journal*, July 9, 2009. Reprinted by permission of "How to Make a Fortune from the Biggest Bailout in U.S. History," copyright © 2009 Dow Jones & Company, Inc. All Rights Reserved Worldwide. License number 2256050755971.

p. 183 Hut community, courtesy MARKA/Alamy.